Hans-Jürgen Wirth
9/11 as a Collective Trauma

SERIES »PSYCHE AND SOCIETY«
EDITED BY JOHANN AUGUST SCHÜLEIN
AND HANS-JÜRGEN WIRTH

Hans-Jürgen Wirth

9/11
AS A COLLECTIVE
TRAUMA

AND OTHER ESSAYS ON
PSYCHOANALYSIS AND SOCIETY

Psychosozial-Verlag

Distributed in the USA, Canada and South America by
THE ANALYTIC PRESS,
101 West Street, Hillsdale,
New Jersey, 07642, USA.
E-Mail: orders@analyticpress.com

©2004 Psychosozial-Verlag
Goethestr. 29, D-35390 Gießen.
Tel.: +49 641 77819; Fax: +49 641 77742
www.psychosozial-verlag.de
E-Mail Publisher: info@psychosozial-verlag.de
E-Mail Author: hjw@psychosozial-verlag.de
Cover: German poster towards the end of WW II calling for the
darkening of windows during air raids (detail)
Cover layout: Christof Röhl
based on a draft by Atelier Warminski, Büdingen
Layout: Till Wirth based on a draft by Peter Großhaus
Printed by Majuskel Medienproduktion GmbH,
www.digitalakrobaten.de
ISBN 0-88163-434-4

TABLE OF CONTENTS

PREFACE

Psychoanalysts and psychologists are generally not asked for advice on politics, power, terrorism and war. Military experts as well as scientists of political science and Islam, journalists, diplomats and the secret service are responsible for these issues — and if a child has already fallen into the well, historians will be asked.

On the one hand, the injured child, the traumatized people and the scared population are indeed areas which psychoanalysts, psychotherapists, social workers and psychologists, child and youth psychotherapists and volunteers are sent to. Their job is to undo what cannot be undone. These attributes apply all over the world. Sometimes the members of these psychosocial professions agree with this description of their work: They do not feel responsible for such obscene issues as power, threats of violence and terror.

On the other hand, there is hardly any other group in society which has the same intimate knowledge as psychosocial professions of the psychological and social background and the consequences of violence, war and terror. Their experiences emphasize that the economical, power-political and military explanations of terrorism and war are not thorough enough if they leave out the psychological dimension. Considering the background and the consequences of terrorism as well as the American reaction to terrorism, the psychological aspects are much more important than most politicians are willing to accept.

All the more, the psychological perspective gains more importance if one deals with humanitarian problems. The psychotherapeutic sphere is one of the few fields in society in which the ideas of being a human being are openly discussed and proved of their validity. The vision of humanitarian conditions and standards are not created in an environment where everything is better, faster, higher, not where it is prettier and more aesthetic, and not even where it is peaceful and harmonic, but they are developed through dealing with the dark sides of life, with illness, pain, suffering, traumatic experiences, farewell, mourning and death. Therefore, psychotherapy is one of the few social fields in which new visions of human culture could be developed.

The attempt to build bridges between politics and what we know from the field of therapy and applied psychoanalysis are currently not especially popular. Psychoanalytic enlightenment collides easily with individual politicians who are interested in having power, because this enlightenment uncovers their strategies of denial and cover-up. In this sense, investigative journalism and psychoanalysis share the same fate. It is difficult for them to convince the public because political leaders do not simply fall into categories of »good« and »evil« but represent, in a certain way, the ideology and defense mechanisms which the population expects of them.

September 11 still has an enormous impact on the thoughts of politicians and society worldwide, consciously and unconsciously. It is also one of the main issues in the media. It is even used to justify a completely new world order. War could have almost become acceptable if in the meantime, all of the fake secret service reports, lies and tricks during the war on Iraq had not become public.

With the help of these collected papers I would like to stimulate the reader to use the psychoanalytic method not only for clinical questions but also for cultural, social, historical and even political problems. I can, therein, rely on Sigmund Freud, who, at the end of his great paper *Civilization and its Discontents* (1930), in the night before the National Socialists came into power raised the question whether »we [may] not be justified in reaching the diagnosis that, under the influence of cultural urges, some civilizations, or some epochs of civilization — possibly the whole of mankind — have become ›neurotic‹?« (ibid., p. 110). As Freud's own works on the psychoanalytic theory of culture show — for instance, his social-psychological analysis about the relationship between the individual, mass, leader and institution which he presented in Mass Psychology and Ego Analysis (1921) and his critical view on religion in *The Future of an Illusion (1927)* — that psychoanalytic knowledge can be transferred successfully to a single phenomenon of culture as well as to the whole culture.

In the course of the medicinalization of psychoanalysis, the culture theory has been neglected. After Freud, the application of psychoanalytic knowledge on social, cultural and political phenomena has remained a ›stepchild‹ of psychoanalysis. Therefore, the situation of psychoanalytic culture theory is ambivalent: On the one hand, the majority of psychoanalysts concentrates on the therapeutic application of psychoanalysis and their interests are focused on purely clinical theories and phenomena. On the other hand, the sciences of culture, society and literature and the social and human sciences have discovered psychoanalysis and used it for their own purpose. One cannot overlook the influence psychoanalysis has had on the sciences of literature, ethnology, sociology, academic psychology, the studies of religion, theology, peace and conflict research, philosophy, qualitative social research, biographical research, political psychology, historical science, theory of art, sexual research, etc. Psychoanalysts did not try to influence these other sciences; rather, the other sciences have used psychoanalysis in order to find explanations for problems in their fields.

As Freud had hoped, a process has taken place in which psychoanalysis »as depth psychology« and as »the teachings of the unconscious« would become indispensable for all sciences which deal with the development of human culture and with its large institutions such as art, religion and social order.

In *The Question of Lay Analysis* (1926, pp. 83 f), Freud writes: »It has already, in my opinion, afforded these sciences considerable help in solving their problems. But these are only small contributions compared with what might be achieved if historians of civilization, psychologists of religion, philologists, and so on would agree themselves to handle the new instrument of research which is at their service. The use of analysis for treatment of the neuroses is only one of its applications; the future will perhaps show that it is not the most important one.«

The answer to the question of which therapeutic effects the psychoanalytic enlightenment has produced is also two-sided. In the beginning, Freud was very skeptical. In *Civilization and its Discontents*, he asked: »[W]hat would be the use of the most correct analysis of social neuroses, since no one possesses authority to impose such a therapy upon the group?« (Freud 1930, S. 505). However, the effects of psychoanalytic analyses on public opinion and the political-cultural climate of a society should not be underestimated. In its discussion, it is not rare that the public resorts to psychoanalytic arguments — whether these are taken from »wild« psychoanalysis (Freud 1910) or not would have to be discussed individually — in order to critically challengepolitical opinions and cultural phenomena of the time. Thus, in the 1960s the book *The Inability to Mourn* (1967) by Alexander und Margarete Mitscherlich had an extraordinary influence on the public discussion within the Federal Republic of Germany about its National Socialist past. At the very least, the dictum of the »German inability to mourn« and the »necessity of going through a mourning process« has become a fixed expression within the discussion of Germany's National Socialist past.

Besides their offer to the readers, the essays in this volume are also meant as an offer to politics. The attempt to perceive and describe reality not only in economic, military, and power-political but also in psychic categories also directs one's attention towards alternative political strategies for action whose practicability seems more plausible — to me, at least — than those which have been discussed and carried out since the attacks on the World Trade Center. The practical therapeutic experiences psychoanalysts have gained in dealing with the unconscious processes of violence, traumatization, destructiveness, self-destructiveness, and the fending-off of these by turning against others in violence could be a reliable foundation on which to deal constructively with the processes of collective violence.

Hans-Jürgen Wirth, Giessen and New York City, July 2004

9/11 AS A
COLLECTIVE TRAUMA[1]

>The fateful question for the human species seems to me to be whether and to what extent their cultural development will succeed in mastering the disturbance of their communal life by the human instinct of aggression and self-destruction (...) Men have gained control over the forces of nature to such an extent that with their help they would have no difficulty in exterminating one another to the last man. They know this, and hence comes a large part of their current unrest, their unhappiness and their mood of anxiety.<
Freud (1930), pp. 111 f

>The narcissist must perpetually live with the divine.<
Grunberger & Dessuant (1997/2002), p. 379

The monstrous attack of September 11, 2001 on the World Trade Center in New York and the Pentagon in Washington has — in Freud's words (1930) — once again demonstrated to the entire world how difficult it is for »the human species« to overcome »the disturbance of their communal life by the human instinct of aggression and self-destruction« (p. 111). However, Freud's hypothesis regarding aggression, self-annihilation, or the death instinct must not be truncated to a mono-causal interpretation of destructive action as though the terrorist act against the

---

[1] This article was previously published in Piven, Boyd & Lawton (Eds.). (2002): Jihad and Sacred Vengeance: Psychological Undercurrents of History Volume III. NY: iUniverse and a previous version in: The Journal of Psychohistory. Vol 30 No 4, 2003, 363 – 388.

World Trade Center could be »conceptualized,« explained, or understood simply by reference to aggressive-destructive human instincts.

Instead, the theoretical achievement of Freud's death instinct hypothesis lies in the mere insistence that each of us carries within himself the potential toward destructiveness. The terrorist act of Sept. 11, 2001 is not by any means one of »unimaginable cruelty«, as commentaries have frequently described it. Rather, such a scenario had been painted in detail by creative minds within Hollywood's movie industry years earlier, and a public numbering in the millions came to be entertained, fascinated, and horrified by it. The human destructive potential is ever-present: basically, people are capable of any act of cruelty the human imagination can conjure up. However, to what extent the individual is beset by such destructive instincts and whether the destructive fantasies are acted out or remain within the realm of fantasy depends on many other complexly interlinked conditions — among them, those defined by the concepts of malignant narcissism, delusions of grandeur, feelings of powerlessness,

Max Klinger (1857–1919): Third Future (1880)

individual and collective traumatizations, fanaticism, fundamentalism, and paranoid world views.

Neither are events such as the terror attack of September 11, 2001 »bestial« by the original definition of the word »beast« (wild animal, non-human) but, on the contrary, characteristic of the human species. Animals — barring a few exceptions for the sake of conserving their species — have an instinctual inhibition against killing members of their own kind. Animals are therefore not at all capable of committing any massacre of their own species. This is unique to humans. The potential for committing a monstrous crime is a

Alfred Kubin: War (1903)

fundamental component of the human condition. On the one hand, relative freedom from instinctual behavior holds the potential for freedom and creativity, for free decision-making, while on the other hand, it allows the freedom to choose evil. Without their freedom to choose evil, humans would not be truly free. We cannot have one without the other. »This makes evil the risk and also the price of freedom« (Safranski 1997, p. 193). It does not mean to surrender to evil. Instead, humans are confronted with the difficult task of fighting evil, yet without being able to eliminate it from human life altogether; for all attempts to do so will inevitably bring about further evil, as they prove destructive to freedom.

Freud's pessimistic image of human nature, as expressed in his death instinct hypothesis, refers to the danger that even the victims of destructive force — on September 11, they were Americans — are not immune to becoming »powers of darkness« themselves in their resistance. The tragedy is that the struggle against evil engenders further evil.

The division of the world into rigidly separate categories of pure »good« and »evil« is one of the central psychological conditions for terrorism. Terrorists can only put their superegos out of action by dehumanizing their opponents and equating them with absolute evil. Conversely, in calling for a »battle of good against evil« and even a »crusade against evil«, U. S. President George W. Bush assumes the same mental division that is one of the causes of the problem — not its solution. Because in reality, as Freud (1915) wrote in »Thoughts for the Times on War and Death«,

> »Evil cannot be ›eradicated‹. Psychological — or, to be exact, psychoanalytic — investigation demonstrates instead that the deepest essence of human nature consists of instinctive drives of an elementary nature that are equally inherent in all people and designed for satisfaction of certain basic needs. These instinctive drives are neither good nor evil in themselves (...) A human being is rarely completely good or evil, but mostly ›good‹ in one relationship, ›evil‹ in another, or ›good‹ under certain external circumstances, and under others, decidedly ›evil.‹« (p. 331 f)

Indeed, evil — currently embodied in terrorism — is a hydra: cut off one of her heads, and ten new heads will sprout from the stump (cf. Nitzschke 2001). The equivalent is true for American resistance. Whenever legitimate and necessary resistance itself resorts to terrorist measures and is carried out within the framework of a crusader mentality, it will continuously create its enemies anew while claiming to destroy them. An effective strategy against terrorism must address the glaring inequalities between the First, Second, and Third Worlds *and also fight the psychosocial causes of terrorism* if it is to succeed in the long run.

The Syndrome of Fanaticism

Terrorists, in particular suicide murderers, are fanatics. Even though fanaticism as an individual and collective phenomenon is subject to historical change and is extremely complex (cf. Hole 1995, p. 36), an attempt at a brief definition shall be made here. In his book *Fanatismus* (Fanaticism), Günter Hole (1995) emphasizes the fanatic's »passion« and »rashness«, the basis on which he »uncompromisingly« and »rigidly« defends his »overrated idea« (p. 37):

> »Fanaticism is a personal conviction with a high degree of identification, pertaining to restricting contents and values, and influenced by personality structure; it is maintained or pursued with the greatest intensity, persistence and steadfastness, accompanied by an incapacity for dialogue or compromise with other systems or persons, who may be fought as external enemies by any means necessary and in conformity with the fanatic's own conscience.« (Hole 1995, p. 39)

Wurmser (1989) — citing Haynal and Puymège — summarizes the traits of fanaticism as follows:

> »Belief, an excess of zeal, exclusivity, automatic purity, complete involvement [in an overrated ideology] to the point of suicide and crime, the certainty of possessing *the* truth, the knowledge of good and evil, which are seen as absolute, a dichotomizing, standardizing way of thinking, an aversion to all that is contrary to this truth or would question it, an absolute faith regarding certain ideals as sacred and promising perfection and harmony in this life or beyond, as well as the destruction of what is alien to, or opposes, this faith.« (Wurmser 1989, p. 167)

Erich Fromm (1961) particularly stresses that not every person who has a »profound belief« or has embraced a »philosophical or scientific conviction« must immediately be classified as a fanatic. In fact, the fanatic could be identified »more easily by certain personality traits than by the contents of his convictions« (p. 61). The fanatic, he states, has killed off all feelings for other people and projected them to the party or group whose ideology seems reasonable to him. He deifies the collective and its shared ideology, to which he has become enslaved. His complete submission under this idol creates a passion within him whose emotional quality Fromm characterizes as »cold fire« and »burning ice«, as »passion lacking warmth« (ibid.). The fanatic »acts, thinks and feels on behalf of his idol« (ibid.) and is prepared to sacrifice for it everything he still holds dear in life. For example, the Palestinian Nizzar Iyan confessed in a *Zeit* interview (cf. Schirra 2001) that he found his greatest fulfillment in his sons' sacrifice as suicide murderers in the fight against the Israelis. When his 17-year-old son Ibrahim, whom he had trained as a »killer in the name of God« (p. 15), actually lost his life in a suicide bombing, his father said, »my son Ibrahim is dead. I never felt happier than at the moment when they came and said, ›the Jews killed your son‹.« And when the interviewer asked: »but you, after all, are his father, you must feel pain«, the father replied, unmoved, »I am quite honest, I am saying this out of conviction, I do not feel grief, I feel joy, true joy, that my son has accomplished a part of what we believe in. Life has no savor when one cannot accomplish one's dreams and one's goals« (p. 16).

What Hole (1995) says about the fanatic applies to this Palestinian father: typical fanatics »place ideas above people; their dedication to ideas is abnormally powerful, while their dedication to people is strangely blocked or defective« (p. 93). The fanatic lacks »the capacity for empathy«, for »understanding«, for »sympathy«, which »on principle is based on a capacity for love, for openness, for letting other people come close« (p. 94). The fanatic has submerged his inner emptiness, depression, and despair »in a complete submission to the idol and in the simultaneous idolization of his own self, which he has made a component of the idol. (...) Theoretically speaking, the fanatic is a highly narcissistic personality« (Fromm 1961, p. 61).

By deadening his empathy, his sympathy toward his fellow humans and his libidinous ties to his next of kin, the fanatic has, above all, rid himself of his own feelings, which he fears as the most threatening of all perils. The fanatic panics when faced with all feelings: the »disagreeable« ones of remorse, guilt, shame just as much as the »agreeable« feelings of love, gratitude, being touched and being moved, the feeling of unity. The point is a basic fear of his own emotional inner world, of the depth of his emotional life. Opening up to this world means leaving himself wide open, capable of being touched, and therefore vulnerable. Love is extremely dangerous as it is always related to a type of commitment, a self-exposure to the other, a self-dedication, a loosening of the boundaries around the self, relinquishment of claims to power, and an emotional dependence on the love object. »Fanaticism is always the result of an incapacity for genuine relatedness« (ibid.). Dependence on others and being at the mercy of the inherent dynamism of one's own feelings is felt to be the absolute risk. You must not show feelings! You must not have feelings! You must not let yourself be touched! You must not abandon yourself to feelings of love! You shall believe in the pure doctrine, in your own power, and in the power of your leader and organization alone! You shall love only your leader and the sacred doctrine! — this is what the fanatic's motto might sound like.

This thesis is not invalidated by the fact that some of the terrorists were living in Germany as inconspicuous students, and that at least the terrorist Muhammad Atta had a

Alfred Kubin: Adoration (c. 1900)

girlfriend, who reported to the police that he was missing. However, it is characteristic that he was ready to leave his girlfriend without one word of goodbye and to take off on his deadly mission, knowing it would end in his own death. It is characteristic of fanatics like Atta that they cannot understand anyone else's feelings about »how other people suffer from their conduct and its consequences. They are thus capable of inflicting suffering and pain, or to accept these unmoved as ethically justified and required by the Utopian ideology of the fanatical system« (ibid., p. 94).

On the day of the attacks on the World Trade Center, terrorist pilot Muhammad Atta's luggage, which had not been transferred on time, was found at the Boston Airport (cf. *Der Spiegel* 40/2001, pp. 32 – 33). Among other things, it contained the suicide pilot's last will, a psychologically informative document revealing Atta's inner world. Among the 18 items in his will, three alone dealt with his fear of the impurity of women:

»5. Neither pregnant women nor unclean persons shall say goodbye to me — I disapprove of that.

6. Women shall not apologize for my death (...)

11. Women shall neither be present during the burial nor come to my grave on any occasion thereafter.«

A. Paul Weber: The Damocles Bomb (1972)

Misogyny — in particular, fear of the emancipated, self-confident, sexually active woman — is not merely an individual characteristic of Atta's but a widespread phenomenon in the Islamic world. Within the traditionally patriarchal culture of Islam, the narcissism of Islamic males was enormously inflated by the elevation of males and devaluation of females. Western influence and its egalitarian orientation causes many male Muslims to feel injured in their self-esteem and to seek reassurance in Islamic fundamentalism, which promises them an ego boost by elevating them above women and debasing females, as demonstrated by the Taliban system with graphic clarity. Piven (2002) proposes as a thesis that the extreme social isolation, suppression, humiliation, and physical maltreatment of women which are the norm in many Islamic countries must be regarded as an indirect, psychological cause of terrorism. The women, who have been traumatized by clitoral circumcision, rape, beating, and other physical maltreatment, pass on their own traumas to their children. Suffering from depression, self-mutilation, and other post-traumatic stress symptoms themselves, they visit their humiliations upon their children — not only, but particularly their sons, inducing in them the panic fears which they themselves have suffered. The boys, having been traumatized in that way and burdened with (sexual) anxieties, develop an image of women de-

German poster towards the end of WW II calling for the darkening of windows during air raids (detail)

termined by fear of fusion and longing for fusion, of contempt and hatred, and as soon as they are old enough, take refuge in the world of men, which is strictly separate from that of women. The circle is completed when the men — in order to stabilize their own identities — debase and humiliate their partners just as they have been debased and humiliated by their own traumatized mothers. Due to fear of women, who are fantasized as sadistic (= mother), small boys are often sexually abused by grown men in order to avoid sexual contact with women, who are simultaneously dreaded and despised. As may also be gathered from Osama bin Laden's biography, many fundamentalist men initially viewed the sexual freedom which splashed into some of the Arab nations together with oil dollars and Western culture as a welcome temptation.

However, during a second stage, many reacted with guilt feelings and panic before the revenge of their internalized ter-

Alfred Kubin: Power (1903)

rible mother imagoes. Western civilization came to represent their own »wicked selves« and had to be fought by all means (p. 43). It is no accident that in the terrorists' justifications and accusations, the sexual permissiveness of the West has always played a prominent role.

Fear of fusion with a woman and »the development of armor against women« have been thoroughly described by Klaus Theweleit (1977, 1978) with respect to the personality type of the »military male«. His psychoanalytic-psychohistorical analysis points out the psychological and psychosomatic role played by military battle in relation to the self and the body: on the one hand, military drill promotes the creation of a »body made of steel«, a »body machine«, an Ernst Jünger type of »man of steel« (Theweleit 1978, p. 185), but on the other hand, the »military male« longs for the moment when the body armor is blown open and the rigid body ego (...) disappears« (p. 208):

Being ›cold metal‹ without any feelings, and yet piercing through the twitching bodies — an intoxication with power, with crossing a boundary. The attacking military males are seeking a transformation, a breakout from their selves, by every means. They anticipate this sensation most intensely when, like missiles fired by the military machine, they finally take on the movement of the bullet themselves, racing toward the bodies under attack. The invocation of their own speed, never absent, is needed to render plausible the breakouts, the break-throughs, the contact with the body of the enemy and its penetration ... The break-through occurs not in a state of intense pleasure, but rather, in a state of intense self-observation. Above all, they need their icy-clear minds so that nothing happening to their own bodies might escape them. After all, nothing must happen to this body except when it kills, or when it dies. Icy-cold thinking — awareness of their own bodies during the anticipation of the act of killing, or their own death (I kill, therefore I am. I die, therefore I was.) (pp. 209–223).

Detail from a German poster toward the end of World War II, exhorting people to observe the blackout because of bombing raids. In: Theweleit 1978, p. 209.

Theweleit's remarks may also be read as a possible interpretation of the psychological processes that might have taken place within the terrorist pilots, though with the reservation that we have very little concrete information about what these people felt during their deadly flights. Still, the analogy with Theweleit's »military men« remains striking. According to Hole (1995), the fanatic is distinguished by a »paralysis and rigidity in the affective sphere« (p. 93), complemented by »a troubled relationship with his own body« — indeed, a »marked hostility toward his body«. Hostility toward the body, ideals of purity, a striving for complete spiritualization, devaluation of actual existence, an exaggerated idea of the beyond, the wish to dedicate one's own life completely to an illusionary idea, and finally even to sacrifice one's life: these add up to a characteristic syndrome for all types of fanaticism.

In this respect, Atta's last will also shows agreement with the military man type described by Theweleit: the National Socialists' cult of purity, who fought for the »purity of the Aryan race« and the »purity of the blood«, has its match in the ideal of purity among the Islamic fundamentalists. Item 9 of his will states:

> »9. The person washing my body around my genitals should wear gloves, so that I might not be touched there.« (*Der Spiegel* 40/2001, p. 32)

And the guide for suicide pilots also found in Atta's luggage exhorts them »in the evening, before you commit your act«:

>You must recite that you are dying for God. Shave all superfluous
hair from your body, perfume your body, and wash your body (...)
Cleanse your heart from all bad feelings you might have, and forget
everything related to your worldly existence.« (p. 38)

The fear of death, the fear of the monstrousness of the intended crime, is projected onto the fear of one's own body,
and is exorcised there by cleanliness rituals. These rituals re-
move not only the entire sphere of the physical from reality,
but also the entire »worldly existence«. Along with painstak-
ing cleansing of the body, the »heart is also to be cleansed of
all bad feelings« such as feelings of love, pity, human sympathy, guilt, pangs of conscience, fear of death, feelings of
shame, etc., and the monstrousness of the intended mass
murder must be stripped of actuality. What appears simply
unimaginable becomes an enterprise which, due to its re-
moval from emotional reality and dematerialization, may be
prepared down to its ultimate details.

Grunberger (1984/1989) describes purity as a narcissistic ideal seeking to attain a state of perfection through denial of physical instincts, indeed, through the elimination
of corporeality itself. Grunberger defines purity as an »absolute and autonomous narcissistic ideal (...) from which
the instinctual dimension has been completely eliminat-
ed« (p. 114). Purity is »stripped of every physical element«;
it is unemotional, even »devoid of matter« (p. 116). In
holding up purity as his ideal, the fanatic removes himself
from the real world, which always includes dirt, impuri-
ties, and excrements as components of life, while dedicat-
ing his life to an illusory pure sanctity. In order to imple-
ment his ideal of purity, a projection of the »anality which
is not integrated with the self« onto the external enemies,
who are fantasized as impure, takes place (Grunberger &
Dessuant 1997/2002, p. 272). In wars, particularly those
designated as »holy wars« (»jihad«), the utterly unclean,

the evil, the unbelievers must be exterminated and banned from the world in the name of a »narcissism of purity« (ibid.). The »duo of terror and purity« (Grunberger 1984/1989, p. 119) is found with Robespierre as with the Christians of the Crusades, in Hitler's race doctrine and anti-Semitism, and finally also with the Islamist fanatics.

Consequently, terrorist Atta decreed a prohibition against mourning his death under Item 3 in his will:

> »No one must weep for my sake, cry out, or perhaps rend his garments or strike his face — those are foolish gestures.«

The prohibition against mourning applies not to himself only, but to all others as well. This involves an armor against his own emotions and the emotions of other people, those who are close to him and, all the more, his victims. This mental state is based on a cold façade of invulnerability, rejection, hatred and contempt through establishing the narcissistic counter-ideals of power, control, purity, and unemotionality (cf. Wurmser 1989). Power is worshipped as an absolute value. The terrorist subjects himself to the absolute power of his community and thus achieves narcissistic gratification when the terrorist organization selects him for a suicide attack, providing an immense boost to his feelings of grandiosity. The grandiose self of a terrorist chosen for the task of assuming the role of a holy warrior experiences this like a canonization. A fusion of ego and ego ideal takes place, a submersion of the self in the grandiose self, which is fantasized to be eternal, a reason for regarding his own real death not as a threat but even as salvation. A hate-filled resentment against the enemy makes up the mental structure of the paranoid narcissistic defense, which is directed against humanitarian ideals, libidinous impulses, feelings of grief, and awareness of one's own emotions.

Suicide murderers abandon their selves and become passive instruments of the group they are fighting for. Even so, they are not devoid of conscience but have rigid, overly powerful, fanatical consciences. They believe themselves to be fighting for a good and just cause. Their conscience assigns them the task of dying for their fanatical faith (cf. Hilgers 2001 a,b).

> »To others, the personality shaped by such an ideal may appear ›devoid of conscience‹. In reality, it involves a ruthless inner authority, an inner executioner who judges solely by the criteria of power and powerlessness, purity and contamination, self-assertion and weakness, indeed, judging one's own self like that of everyone else. It is a cruel, categorical conscience — an anal, sadistic, pre-oedipal superego — in which, as it were, the entire trauma of a troubled past resides and keeps on working.« (Wurmser 1989, p. 157 f)

However, fanatics are guided, for the most part, by their ego ideal. Their ego ideal is determined completely by the fundamentalist ideology to which they have dedicated their lives. Thus, Islamists consider the law of the Qur'an to be an embodiment of the absolute good, and the lifestyle of the West an embodiment of absolute evil which must be fought by all means. The objective calls for harming the enemy as much as possible and symbolically injuring, damaging and humiliating him. If this succeeds, the group's objective has been achieved. At that moment, the individual's ideal and the group ideal are in complete harmony. Besides, the reward in store for the suicide murderer who sacrifices his own life is a place in the Beyond.

> »It is the ideal of a person who lives for nothing but power, of someone who can never be moved by feelings, who never shows weakness and uses all other people only as means to the end of asserting his own power, a man of coldness and professional cruelty, without loyalty or love. He is the type of professional warrior and mass murderer (...) In psychoanalytic terminology, this involves a purely narcissistic ideal — an ideal figure which calls for being diametrically opposed to love or any other form of ›weakness‹.« (Wurmser 1989, p. 157)

The Idealization of the Martyr

The fanatic develops a narcissistically overblown self-image, as if he wanted to say: »I am something very special, unusual, unique. I am an angel of light, a savior. I have been endowed with immense power. I don't want people to love me but rather, to admire me or, even better, to fear me. I don't bare my soul to anyone; I show neither feelings nor weakness. That's why I don't depend on anyone. I have everything under control and don't rely on anything or anybody except on the idea which alone leads to salvation and to which I have dedicated myself body and soul. Even though I myself am nothing, I am nevertheless part of a greater, divine power and therefore I may also feel grandiose.«

Kohut (1973) points out that »human aggressiveness (...) is most dangerous when linked to the two great absolutist psychological constellations: the grandiose self and the archaic, almighty object« (p. 533). When the grandiose self in its megalomania and fanaticism is additionally protected and supported by the approval of the archaic almighty object, every self-doubt finally vanishes. This explains why one finds the most horrible destructive force of mankind not in the form of wild, regressive and primitive behavior but in the form of orderly, organized actions during which the perpetrator's destructive aggression has fused with an absolutist conviction of his devotion to an archaic almighty figure (ibid.).

Narcissistic rage may be distinguished from other forms of aggression in that vindictiveness, an inexorable inner drive, an injustice suffered as a narcissistic injury, and shame play a prominent role. There is a »boundless desire to get even with the person inflicting the insult« (p. 536 f.), and the thought process comes »entirely under the domination (...) of the inflated drive« (p. 537).

Over the past decades, a feeling of having been disparaged and humiliated by the West, particularly the United States, has grown in the Islamic World. A fundamental cause is the inconsiderate superpower politics of the United States of America, who parades before other countries as a guardian of human rights, yet does not hesitate to support dictatorial rulers and corrupt regimes whenever this serves its own interests. At the same time, the Islamic World has had to find out that within the context of globalization, their societies and their culture are at the mercy not only of the military-economic superiority of America but even more of the cultural and economic hegemony of the American way of life, which undermines traditional Islamic customs and values. To Islamists, fundamentalism represents an ideological barrier against the cultural pressures of worldwide Americanization. It is directed against the West but also against pro-Western groups and governments inside the Islamic countries themselves.

Within groups in the Islamic World who experience this narcissistic insult with particular intensity, the humiliations have led to narcissistic rage, the extreme expression of which may even assume a form which Hans Magnus Enzenberger (*Frankfurter Allgemeine Zeitung* of 09/18/2001) has termed »Pride in their own Decline«. As Altmeyer (2001) stresses, Enzenberger has thus pointed out the narcissistic origins of this murderous and suicidal destructiveness:

>»Prior to self-annihilation there is the expanding idea of their own greatness: the world shall finally recognize the greatness of their own ideology, their own religion, their own culture, their own race, how outstanding the individual or the collective in themselves is — and they'll be sorry if they don't. The world must all the more urgently recognize their narcissistically inflated grandiosity the more reservations of their own they have already developed about it (...) From this disastrous mixture of self-doubt, insult, and compensatory megalomania results not only the obsessive vision of theocracy. It also nourishes that fatal development which leads to murderous and suicidal terrorism. It is something like a collective narcissistic rage increased to gigantic proportions that we witness in terrorist manifestations of evil.« (p. 13)

How to become a terrorist?

People whose entire lives have been molded by violence and hatred tend towards the assumption that the entire world is structured according to the victim-oppressor model and that it is therefore better to be an oppressor than a victim. As is known from the biographies of criminals convicted of violent crimes, they have often themselves been the victims of physical mistreatment and sexual abuse during their childhood and youth. We know a few things about the suicide murderers among the Palestinians. In particular, the young people who volunteer for

suicide attacks have been subjected to constant traumatization from childhood. Throughout their lives they have
experienced extreme forms of violence, powerlessness,
helplessness and hopelessness. This has desensitized
them. Since not only many individuals have been traumatized but also the collective identity of the group, both the
individual and the collective identity decline into fanaticism. For future fanatics who were not accepted into the
terrorist groups as children, the adolescent phase offers
particularly good conditions for starting such a terrorist
»career« (Büttner 2001, p. 59) since adolescents must
loosen their family ties and are particularly susceptible to
the guidance offered by radicalized groups during their
search for new cultural ideals and values. The virtual biography of a fanatic who is celebrated by the larger group as
its mythical hero serves as a model biography for the adolescents which helps them mold their identities and orient
themselves. At the same time, identification with such culturally prescribed heroes allows them to forge the necessary link between their personal identities and the social
and cultural identity.

They receive a group identity that revolves around fanaticism as its central element. They cannot keep themselves, their families, and their fellow-sufferers from being
constant victims and witnesses of violence. However, they
can ward off their feelings of powerlessness, helplessness,
and hopelessness through counter-violence, through fanaticism, and through a firm belief in an eternal life in the
Beyond and the narcissistic fame of having sacrificed
themselves for the collective. In this situation, fanaticism
appears to them as their last means of salvation. However
wretched, miserable, and bleak their own lives might be,
an absolute identification with the ideals of the group
compensates the individuals for their disgrace. »Group

narcissism«
(Fromm 1964, pp. 199-223; 1973, pp. 179-184) provides an important prop for an individual's feeling of self-worth, and in the event of collective insults may become a source of aggression and fanaticism.

Some of today's Islamist terrorists and Al Qaeda fighters may have been traumatized in refugee camps, recruited there by the various secret services, and raised and educated in special Qur'an schools and training camps. Others are conscripted by the terrorist organizations as »young people between the ages of 18 and 28, single, no children, without obligations to family« (Hirschmann 2001, p. 12) and schooled and indoctrinated in training camps. »It is an open secret« that even »in Gaza and in Western Jordan there are places where young Palestinians are instructed by teachers in the discipline of suicide killing« (Schirra 2001, p. 15). In the monastic solitude of such camps, the community functions as a family substitute and their fanatical leaders function as substitute parent figures so that children and adolescents develop an intense emotional and

intellectual dependency which makes them susceptible to
fanaticism. These child soldiers are inoculated with a fundamentalist, diminished form of Islam and programmed
for their mission. By such methodical indoctrination, fanatics are raised who are members of a sect they neither
wish to leave nor would be able to leave (cf. Lachkar
2002). On the one hand, the honor of being chosen for
the sacred mission of sacrificial death provides tremendous narcissistic gratification, while on the other, every as-
pirant beset by doubts and anxieties must fear the dispar-
agement and humiliation of the group and the leader —
or worse. All of the mostly young Palestinian suicide murderers (»shahid«) who have blown themselves up are ven-
erated as the »war dead of God« (p. 16). »Palestinian Television is sending advertising spots concerning ›our dead
heroes‹, and its newspapers applaud the ›fight for Palestinian freedom‹. Photos of the dead, blood-red, almost
kitschy, are assembled into a gallery of death« (ibid.).
While the holy warrior who sacrifices his life for the ideology of the sect is promised that he will immediately go to
heaven, traitors are threatened with a shameful death.
During the recruiting process, future suicide murderers are
systematically exposed to extreme psychological and physical stresses reminiscent of brainwashing, torture, and »artificial« traumatization methods. Thus the Palestinian
Eyad Saradsh, who runs a psychiatric center in Gaza, reports that the candidates »had to sit in a room silently and
completely isolated for days, or spend 48 hours underground inside a grave next to a corpse« (quoted by Luczak
2001, p. 89). Such extreme stress leads to renewed traumatization accompanied by intense feelings of fear, shame,
narcissistic depreciation, helplessness and powerlessness.
The obvious alternative is unreserved identification with
the group, its leader, and the group's ideology. The result

is a fanatical adherent, a holy warrior, who can find everything that's »good« exclusively in the ideology of the sect, and who has projected everything »bad« and hateful onto the enemy.

This dynamic applies in particular to people living in refugee camps under miserable conditions for several generations, who are traumatized by the everyday presence of violent behavior. However, the New York assassins were not Palestinians but well-educated students, including some from the United Arab Emirates. Osama bin Laden hails from Saudi Arabia, one of the wealthiest countries in the world.

As Kernberg (2002) emphatically stresses, traumatization results not only from violence experienced by one's own body but also from violent acts one has witnessed. If someone is forced to watch helplessly and passively while a person dear to him suffers violence, injustice and humiliation, this too may be experienced as a trauma. Such forms of terror were known during the ethnic cleansing by the Serbs in Kosovo when men had to watch their wives being raped, or women had to watch their husbands being murdered. Analogous processes involving Palestinians have been going on in the Near East for decades. Through their collective identity, the Arabs and Muslims in the Arabic countries feel close to the suffering of the Palestinian people. They sympathize (= suffer) with the Palestinians and have developed a collective hatred of Israel and the United States, and in part also of the Western World as a whole. Because of their strong collective identity, many Muslims feel »traumatized as a collective — even if they come from a middle-class environment in relatively moderate Egypt, as did Muhammed Atta« (Luczak 2001, p. 86). Some individuals may feel a particular duty to support the Palestinians in their strug-

gle against Israel and its powerful protector, the U.S.,
precisely due their privileged position. It is even conceivable that in an exceptional case, a terrorist career may
start with genuine human feelings of responsibility and
solidarity, only to develop into fanatical hatred over the
course of the years. Even the German terrorists of the
Rote-Armee-Fraktion (RAF), who launched attacks on
symbolic representatives of the government and the capi-
talist economic system during the 1970s were people
who had been motivated by high moral principles and
involved in various public-spirited projects before their
violent activities. As I have argued elsewhere (cf. Wirth
2001a, b, 2002), the RAF terrorists were »unconscious
delegates« (Stierlin 1978) of their parents and their generation. In a certain sense, they did not act voluntarily
but unconsciously, on their parents' behalf, caught up in
a trans-generational conflict. They targeted the wrong
object at the wrong time, but they were attempting to
make up for their parents' generation's failure to resist a
regime of terror during the period of National Socialism.

The Islamic terrorists joining the holy war are often
caught up in a similar generational context in that, on the
one hand, the privileged and affluent Arabic families live
in almost unimaginable oil prosperity and enjoy the luxu-
ry of Western industrial society, yet, on the other hand,
they ideologically support hatred against the West and solidarity with the Palestinian people. This double standard
presents a difficult conflict in the clash between the generations which is resolved when the sons of economically
privileged families, at the conscious or unconscious bid-
ding of their parents, join the holy war which their fathers
only speak and dream of. Indeed, after September 11,
much information has been found about terror groups,
»jihadists«, that is, »professional fanatics using religion as

an argument« (Hirschmann 2001, p. 14) being financially supported by numerous Islamic businessmen who successfully pursue their business in Europe and the United States and salve their Islamic consciences through such donations. Even — and particularly — in Saudi Arabia, the extended ruling royal family provides numerous Islamic terror organizations with considerable financial means in order to buy off its moral and political responsibility.

September 11, 2001 as a Collective Trauma

In addition to the psychology of the terrorists, the psychological condition of the Americans exposed to collective traumatization on September 11 is of far-reaching significance for world politics. A trauma is an experience of such intensity that it overwhelms the mind's capability for dealing with it. The trauma is accompanied by feelings of extreme fear — frequently, fear of death —, terror, powerlessness, and total hopelessness. This leads to a collapse of central functions of the self and a fundamental shock to the entire personality. If this happens to a large group of people at once, it is called »collective trauma«. Undoubtedly, the destruction of the World Trade Center in New York and the partial destruction of the Pentagon represent a collective traumatization of the American nation which has left America's collective sense of identity and group narcissism profoundly shaken. This applies not only to people who lost relatives, friends, and acquaintances but to the collective as a whole.

As a result of the terrorist attack on their metropolis and the symbol of its economic and technical superiority, the United States as a world power was confronted with the experience of vulnerability, the finality of life, and help-lessness in the face of »evil«. What did not agree with the conception of the world and self-image of America at all became a terrifying, yet irrefutable reality: even the super-power of America may be harmed. Neither their secret services, the FBI and CIA, equipped though they are with the latest computers, nor their atomic weapons could protect the United States from this attack — to say nothing of the nuclear shield. At the same time, the catastrophe caused a wave of mourning, sympathy, and readiness to help. Still, the question remains whether the Americans will be able to successfully work their way through the suffered trauma. In the last chapter of my book »Narcissism and Power« (Wirth 2002, pp. 381 f.), written in December 2001, I made a prediction which has unfortunately come true. I stated:

> »Should the Americans not succeed in collectively dealing on a psychological level with the trauma they have suffered, they will risk developing a post-traumatic stress syndrome which could manifest itself through constant reliving of the traumatic event, as a mental fixation on the trauma, as uncontrolled panic attacks, and as equally violent and abrupt outbursts of aggression against others. American society might be tempted to ward off the collective trauma by fixating on the trauma and making it the central reference point of its national identity. As a ›selected trauma‹ — as Vamik Volkan calls it — it would be constantly present and provide steady justification for the country's own paranoid aggressive attitudes. America would endlessly have to prove its military superiority by — more or less randomly — defining enemies, pursuing, and annihilating them. This might finally lead to a nationalistic ideology including delusions of persecution, revenge, and grandeur. Their function would be to compensate for the humiliation and narcissistic injuries to the feeling of self-worth by revenge. If society authorizes a leader to organize a campaign of revenge, the politician who champions the paranoid ideology with the greatest fanaticism, and most fervently promises to take revenge for the sake of compensatory justice in order to restore the shaken self-image of grandeur, will enjoy the highest standing«.

Psychodynamic connections of this kind may well have been on the mind of Arundhati Roy (2001), one of the most prestigious and successful Indian writers, when in her commentary »Terrorism is a Symptom, not the Disease«, she compared Osama bin Laden and George W. Bush. Her article caused a worldwide sensation — in the Western countries, mostly outrage — and in Germany, almost led to the resignation of the popular news anchorman Ulrich Wickert because he had cited Roy's ideas approvingly in a magazine article.

First of all, it is interesting that Roy uses a psychological and medical metaphor in distinguishing between »symptom« and »disease«. She even explicitly refers to »family dynamics«:

> »What is Osama bin Laden? He's America's family secret. He is the American president's dark doppelgänger. The savage twin of all that purports to be beautiful and civilized. He has been sculpted from the spare rib of a world laid to waste by America's foreign policy: its gunboat diplomacy, its nuclear arsenal, its vulgarly stated policy of ›fullspectrum dominance‹ (...) Now that the family secret has been spilled, the twins are blurring into one another and gradually becoming interchangeable (...) Now Bush and Bin Laden have even begun to borrow each other's rhetoric. Each refers to the other as ›the head of the snake‹. Both invoke God and use the loose millenarian currency of good and evil as their terms of reference.«

In the 09/15/2001 issue of *Der Spiegel* (38/2001), that is, only four days after September 11 and still before the publication of Roy's article, German Journalist Henryk M. Broder launched a vehement attack against an argumentation he considered a »playing down of Islamic terrorism« and »the inclination to murder«. His comments read like an advance criticism of Roy. Broder believes that many European intellectuals tend to »soft-pedal terror.« This, he said, was the expression of a »post-liberal and pre-suicidal position«:

»We Westerners see no problem with condemning the fanaticism of Christians and Jews; only with fanatical Muslims do we incline toward a position that is normally assumed toward small children and full-grown autists: They know not what they do, but somehow they mean well.« (p. 169)

Broder is apparently of the opinion that it is neither necessary nor appropriate to put oneself into the minds of the assassins or even to look for concrete causes, motives and backgrounds for terrorism:

»Samuel Huntington was right: this involves a struggle of cultures. Global justice is not an issue, and neither are the legitimate rights of the Palestinians, nor those of any other oppressed people; it is purely a matter of the desire to kill, which by now does not even need a pretext.« (p. 169)

Apart from the fact that »the desire to kill« represents, among other things, a psychological motive — which, psychoanalytically speaking, derives from a personality model based on psychological drives —, Broder may be criticized for unthinkingly equating the effort for psychological understanding of the perpetrators' mental condition with secret approval for their deeds.

But even Roy does not seem to understand all the implications of her argumentation using relationship dynamics. To continue with the family dynamics metaphor used by Roy, one could object to her argumentation by saying that many symptoms and many carriers of symptoms are so dangerous that one must fight them by radical means. A relationship-oriented or family dynamic-based perspective does not necessarily exclude treatment methods that would limit freedom. Even if family dynamics may provide information as to why a young killer became a killer, and by the logic of relationship dynamics in a certain sense »inevitably« so, this does not preclude that he is the one who must be held responsible and placed behind bars — not his parents, even though their unconscious conflicts have contributed their share to making him a killer. Besides, a large part of medicine and also psychotherapy is directed primarily toward the symptoms and only secondarily toward the prevention of future pathologies. With life-threatening symptoms in particular, the medical doctor and the therapist will concentrate their efforts toward treating, limiting, and fighting the symptoms, and only after these are held in check, will their attention shift toward preventive measures. Thus, even a perspective based on family dynamics may well result in treating individual family members by different methods and in different settings. Frequently, with exceptionally severe family pathologies, hospital treatment of a particular family member — perhaps an anorexic daughter — is started first, and only after family conflicts have settled down somewhat, a family-therapeutic dialogue as such may begin for treating the cause and for prevention.

How, then, should one deal with fanatics and terrorists, and how should action be taken against them? Individual terrorists and terrorist groups can be tracked down militarily and wiped out. Yet, terrorism is primarily a »communicative strategy« whose aim is the »provocation of power« (Waldmann 1998, p. 13). Terrorism is the weapon of the powerless. Terrorists are fanatics who pursue a communicative strategy to deal with their opponents and with the public, and in the case of September 11 used »the whole world as their sounding board« (Waldmann 2001, p. 4), while at the same time not allowing themselves to be influenced by communication, or only to a very limited degree. Their fanaticism and their paranoid »fortress mentality« shield them against attempts to influence them. In the same way that during family therapy, a »paranoid fortress family« often proves »therapy-resistant« (Richter 1970, p.

224), diplomatic initiatives generally meet with insurmountable obstacles in the case of fanatical and paranoid political and religious groups. One can negotiate with fanatics either not at all or only in a very limited way. Opposing them increases their narcissistic rage just as much as would accommodation or an attempt to soften their positions through negotiation. Their inability to compromise makes them incapable of politics.

In dealing with terrorists, it is, above all, necessary to avoid »traps of countertransference« (Kernberg 1975/1980). One must neither be carried away into reacting vengefully and furiously nor be misled into underestimating the terrorists' viciousness. One must on no account allow the terrorists to dictate the logic of one's actions by unconsciously taking on their paranoid worldview and becoming a player in their resentment and aggression-charged interaction pattern. In addition, victims of violence must beware of identifying with the aggressor. Should Americans engage in such identification with the aggressor, they would adapt to the fanaticism of the terrorists and, to an extent, become fanatical haters themselves, launching a battle against evil without regard for the consequences. It might even happen that the American government might identify with the terrorists in this way and retaliate on the same level and by the same methods. In that case, its military actions would not be guided by a military logic but occur for the sake of psychic stabilization. The purpose of retaliation would not be to strike the »real« opponent but to restore the narcissistic feeling of invulnerability. The objective military function of the military actions would be secondary to their psychological importance: that of making up for the narcissistic injury.

Which answer to terrorism America will choose depends on how the Americans will deal with the trauma they have suffered. George W. Bush accepted the news of the catastrophe with an expressionless face and did not show any irritation, quite in contrast to Bill Clinton, who, in a television interview directly after the attacks, seemed downright shaken. This total separation or suppression of spontaneous feelings is not exactly a sign of success in dealing with trauma; on the contrary: to overcome trauma, it is necessary to go through the phase of depression and sadness. It must be admitted, not repressed. America must attempt to psychically integrate the events. It will take a long grieving process which will occupy America — but also the global public — for weeks, months, probably even years. The grief, despair, anger, and diffuse feeling of powerlessness must be discussed publically as well. With Bush, there is a risk that he might attempt to ward off the trauma through his campaign of punishment and revenge.

The World Trade Center is a symbol of the economic and technical superiority of the United States, the Pentagon of its military might, and Camp David, evidently the goal of the fourth, crashed plane, is a symbol of the peace process — apparently, the terrorists' third symbolic main target. The fact that Camp David was saved from the planned terror attack might be interpreted by the government as a sign that the peace process cannot be destroyed even through this terror attack. However, this would also call for a commitment on the part of America as the last remaining world power to support peace by all available means. It would, above all, apply to the escalation of violence between Israel and Palestine. During his term in office, Clinton personally sought to bring about a reconciliation, but as an outgoing President, he probably lacked the power and conviction. Meanwhile, Bush has arrogantly announced that he was going to pay more attention to American interests, and withdrawn from the mediator role.

George Bush: On a mission from God

Before 9/11, Bush seemed to be a weak president. His democratic legitimization was on shaky grounds. It was not quite clear whether he would be able to step out of his father's shadow. American newspapers printed countless jokes about Bush's visible flaws. These jokes included bashes on his incompetence to improvise when addressing the public, his awkwardness, and his lack of worldly experience. This changed drastically after 9/11. 9/11 gave his dull presidency a higher meaning. When Bush made the decision to go to war, he was finally taken seriously. Bush took his private need to be taken seriously to formulate a maxim for his policy: the world should take *America* seriously again. In Bush's eyes, Clinton had been a weak leader who was responsible for the reason why the world was laughing at America. Bush said in an interview: »I think that people had the idea of an impotent America — a weak, you know, technologically efficient, but not an especially strong country. In the world there is the idea that America has no values and that we will not defend ourselves if we are attacked« (Woodward 2003).

Bush wanted to replace the weak-willed image of America with the image of a powerful and forceful America. He was always determined to take over the role as a rescuer of America's honor and saw the chance of a lifetime to be known in history as a significant president. 9/11 became the »chosen trauma« and was the most important issue in the world. There were no thoughts other than those of revenge and retaliation. The passively suffered trauma was to be retaliated in order to make others the victim of a trauma. If this concept influences America's political and military decisions, America will not really win back its sovereignty;

rather, it will be caught up in a narcissistic collusion with its enemy. Bush's decision to go to war with Iraq was unconsciously influenced by his collusive partner Osama bin Laden. The unconscious dynamics of the relationship between George W. Bush and Osama bin Laden follows the pattern of a narcissistic collusion. The Americans, who are armed to the teeth with weapons, are confronted with a fast, treacherous and invisible enemy who operates in dishonest ways from secret hideouts. The terrorists' intention is to provoke the Americans with terrorist attacks, threats and alarming videotapes in order to cause a military overreaction. They want to involve America in a war, wherever and however possible. The Americans decided to go to war against Iraq even though nearly all of the other nations were against it. The Americans did not listen to the advice of their friends and allies and they did not obey the United Nations because they were solely interested in their narcissistic revenge. They fell into the »relationship trap« and therefore did exactly what the terrorists wanted them to do.

The war in Afghanistan destroyed the Taliban regime and forced many of the Al Qaeda fighters out of their hideouts. The triumph of this victory did not give the Americans enough peace of mind as the U.S. military was unable to capture their leader, Osama bin Laden, »dead nor alive«. Hence, the narcissistic wounds were not healed at all through this military action. Therefore, Bush looked for another enemy, one he thought he would be able to catch, and immediately thought of Saddam Hussein, whose name was already brought up on the evening of September 11. Saddam Hussein, at last, seemed to be easily locatable and perfectly fit the role of the bad guy. Therefore, his regime had to suffer. Besides, the displacement

from Osama bin Laden to Saddam Hussein allowed Bush
to get even with Hussein for trying to murder his father
several years before.

Bush is convinced that his presidency is part of God's
plan. His belief in God's divinity gives him certainty and
devotion. »We do not know the ways of certainty, but we
can trust in it«, said Bush when he addressed the nation.
Bush, who is known for getting up early every day, reads
his prayer book every morning, and his first official act is
to be informed of terrorist threats by the Secret Service.
His beloved God and the evil terrorists are his source of
inspiration. His simple devoutness is not only a private
quirk but also part of his political stance. It is a ritual in
the White House to open cabinet meetings with a prayer.
The closer the Iraq war came, the more forceful his
rhetoric mentioning of God became. Bush is »on a mission from God«, as the German magazine *Der Spiegel*
wrote on its cover. His black-and-white thinking is one of
a fanatic teetotaler. The splitting of good and evil gives
him power and shape. Bush has the personal characteristics which are typical of many dry alcoholics: self-discipline, a strict diet, dedication to sports, an imperturbable
belief in God, and the strict division of the world into
good and evil. Bush speaks openly about his earlier tendency to drink alcohol and to party excessively which he
has now overcome: »You know that I had an alcohol problem. If everything had continued in that way, I would be
sitting in a bar in Texas now instead of the Oval Office.
There is only one reason why I am here in the Oval Office
and not in a bar: I found God.« On his fortieth birthday
he had his first rebirth and swore never to drink alcohol
and party again. The defense mechanism of splitting into
the absolute opposites of good and evil, addiction and
self-discipline, God and terrorism, »the coalition of the

willing« and the »axis of evil« distinguish his views of the world. Bush stated: »This will be a monumental fight between those who are good and those who are evil. But the good will come out on top« (Woodward 2003, p. 61). Not only the terrorists but the American government as well has fallen into fanaticism, which is characterized by a narcissistic self-concept — as if Bush were to say: America is something very special, unusual, one of a kind. It is God's own country. America is equipped with immeasurable power. That is the only thing that matters. The world should not love us but admire us or, even better, fear us. America will not be vulnerable anymore or show any weaknesses. It will only trust its own power. America is suspicious and even looks at its friends and closest allies condescendingly or with disdain. Who is not on our side is against us. If they do not support us, we will buy them. If they are not »for sale«, we will push them to the side as if they were irrelevant. America certainly doesn't depend on anyone. America has everything under control and does not trust in anything and anyone except its own military and economical power. Bush has devoted himself to this idea, which is the only concept he believes in. Early on, it was important for Bush not to let other countries make up the conditions of the war. »It is possible«, he said, »that we will be the only ones left over. I have nothing against it. We are America« (Woodward 2003, p. 98).

How patients in Germany reacted to 9/11

In a certain sense the terror attacks struck not only New York and not only America but the entire world. The commentaries mentioned an »attack on civilization«, and there were assertions that »nothing was the same« after September 11.

Does September 11 truly represent an important geopolitical break? Or did these speeches only pursue a rhetoric of solidarity and a strategy of dramatization in order to line up America's allies and ensure the support of the »anti-terror coalition« for American military action?

Indeed, the American government took the time to prepare the military campaign against the terrorist Al Qaeda network and the Taliban regime in Afghanistan strategically and, above all, diplomatically. In any case, the immediate, overhasty military strike many had expected and feared, which would have been a sign of an uncontrolled, narcissistic, furious reaction, did not occur. This gave the Americans, but also the worldwide public, the opportunity to allow the terror attack in its gigantic dimensions to affect them emotionally.

I believe I can tell from my patients' reactions that their emotional distress was very deep as it impressed and shook most people and undermined their sense of security to a greater extent than any other catastrophe of the last decades. Within the therapeutic setting it is rare for political events to take up so much room. When patients talk about current political events during the therapy hour, they generally do so only if this event is very significant to them personally. It hardly ever happens that a certain political or social event becomes a topic during many therapies. This is due to the »stimulus shield« provided by the therapeutic situation, which prevents current external influences from reducing the patients' concentration on their internal world. While following the reactor catastrophe at Chernobyl, such intense fears were unleashed in many people that they sought therapeutic help (cf. Wirth 1996). Yet the topic only came up in some of the ongoing therapies. The same applies to the Gulf War (cf. Wirth 1991). The terror attacks of September 11, however, went past the stimulus shields of the therapeutic situation in the case of numerous patients.

To a particular degree, this is true of people living in the immediate vicinity of the catastrophe. New York psychoanalyst Irene
Cairo-Chiarandini (2001) reports that she found out about the
catastrophe from one of her patients:

> »It was my third session. The patient, whose body language in the waiting
> room already told me that something terrible had happened, came in,
> stopped in the middle of the office and said, shaken, ›I did not know if you
> wanted me to come.‹ My surprised face — I gradually understood that what-
> ever it was that bothered her also included me — and my slight hand mo-
> tion toward the couch in asking her ›Why shouldn't I?‹ shocked her, since
> she became aware that I did not know and she must tell me. The otherwise
> eloquent, intense woman stuttered and was at a loss for words, in particular
> of the word for ›towers‹. She said with surprising grotesqueness, with a kind
> of functional aphasia, ›Terrorists in airplanes attacked them, the, the, what's
> their name again!!! The ... tall buildings!‹ I helped her through the session. It
> was not until the next session that I found the inner strength to speak of the
> obvious, namely, the reversal of roles, her wish to protect me, her panic that
> she did not know if I would be able to help her.« (p. 36)

Very likely, the patient was not only terribly afraid that the
analyst might not be able to help her but above all, because she could not imagine how the analyst would react:
whether she would lose her composure, whether she —
the patient — would have to support the analyst, or
whether the entire analytical situation would fall apart under the assault of external reality.

I experienced what may be termed the reverse situation
with one of my patients. I had found out about the events in a
break between two therapy sessions. When the patient came
in, I did not notice anything unusual about her and immediately assumed that she did not yet know of the occurrence. I
wondered if I should tell her but decided not to do so. In ret-
rospect, I would have felt better knowing that I had told her
and that perhaps we had talked about it. But at that point in
time I still felt so overwhelmed by the event, and so incapable
of intellectually categorizing its possible effects and emotionally processing them, that I preferred not to talk about it with

the patient. During the following session it was possible to speak of the terror attacks and their effects.

I shall briefly describe several other typical reactions I was able to observe with my patients. One patient who had her therapy session in the evening of September 11 reported that she had immediately felt a severe stomach ache on hearing the news. The next day, a patient said that he had »trembled all over his body« when he learned of the catastrophe. Over the next few days, reactions became even more varied. One patient initially needed to pull himself together in order to voice the opinion that the Americans were now »paying for their arrogant policies«. This was a masochistic, aggression-inhibited patient who generally has a very difficult time in voicing his aggressive feelings. Under the impact of the terror attacks, his usually repressed sadistic impulses were stimulated to such an extent that they were expressed through this opinion, and he apparently identified partially with the terrorists' sadistic position.

A 51-year-old patient, an airplane pilot, appeared almost completely unaffected by the catastrophe. He minimized its significance and considered the American military response and the worldwide reverberation in the media »exaggerated«. In my interpretation, the patient, whose father had committed suicide when the boy was ten years old, believed his narcissistic boundaries to be so threatened by the terror's destructiveness, which reminded him of the destructiveness in his own life, that he had to play down the drama of the events. In addition, his professional activity as a pilot was the only area in his life in which he felt truly secure and competent and which he subsequently sought to protect through narcissistic denial.

A 43-year-old patient spoke of America for an entire therapy session. He remembered having admired and idealized the U.S. as a teenager. When years later, he fulfilled his wish of hearing the »Stones« live in New York, he had, on the one hand, been sobered and repelled by the extensive police controls at the concert, but on the other hand, he had quickly felt at home in Manhattan. He had developed a personal relationship toward the two towers of the World Trade Center and therefore had been »downright wounded« when he had had to witness their destruction on the screen.

The psychological meaning of 9/11 for the entire world

With about half of my patients, the events of September 11 came up as a topic in the therapy sessions. This is something I had never experienced before, not even with Chernobyl, the Gulf War, or changes in government. The enormously broad spectrum of emotional reactions evident in these few patients shows that apparently for many people the »view of the collapsing towers was an intrusion into their private world« (Sznaider 2001, p. 25). Yet in spite of being highly affected emotionally, these people did not let themselves be compelled to react exclusively with moral indignation but also allowed themselves to have spontaneous sensations not considered »politically correct«. The secret sympathy with the terrorists, which may be glimpsed in many statements, is reminiscent of the Mescalero's »clandestine joy« (German: *klammheimliche Freude*; Mescalero was the pseudonym of a leftist student who expressed sympathy for the RAF). I think this does not involve any liking for methods of terrorism, but rather the dim recognition that the »secret power of the powerless and the repressed power of the powerful are linked in an inscrutable mutual dependency« (Richter 2002, p. 16). Arundhati Roy's words that George W. Bush and Osama bin Laden resembled one another like twins hit the nail on the head exactly. Only by perceiving the »mutuality of the suffering both inflict on each other« (Roy 2001) would they be able to recognize their collusive interrelationship — and dissolve it. Natan Sznaider (2001) compares the social thematic focus on the terror attacks with the commemorative culture of the Holocaust: »The Holocaust represents the breach of civilization in modern times, and the borderline between it and barbarism« (p. 28). An equal function could also be claimed for the terror attacks. Both offer an opportunity for civilization: just as the greater part of humanity agrees in regarding the Holocaust as a »breach of civilization«, the quintessential crime against humanity, the world public, in view of the evaluation of the crime committed in New York, might also agree on choosing September 11 as a symbol for the necessity of a global ethics. Such an ethics would commit all peoples, nations and states to develop a new culturally comprehensive self-concept in order to safeguard the future of all humanity. In practical terms, this would mean that the establishment of an international court of law should rapidly go forward.

At the moment it is Americans, most of all, who must learn to understand how vulnerable they are — even, and particularly, as a world power. If the United States assumes that it is immortal, invulnerable, and independent of other nations, it — the greatest economic and military power in the history of mankind — will be subject to a collective narcissistic delusion of grandeur. In fact, even the mightiest power of the world depends on other nations and must adapt to communicating and working together with the losers on the margin of the world. Just as individuals have to accept their own mortality, the collective also faces the task of recognizing its finality and vulnerability to obtain a realistic worldview. Narcissistic injuries are hard to bear, hard to accept, and even traumatizing, but they always involve opportunities to learn something about ourselves and our relationship with the world. The terrible events of September 11 might lead America to the insight that it must relinquish its self-idolization. The enormous economic, military, political, and cultural might at America's disposal is in a dialectic relationship with respect to powerlessness: the more progressive the scientific-technical development, the more grand the successes in subduing nature and man appear, the more complex — and therefore

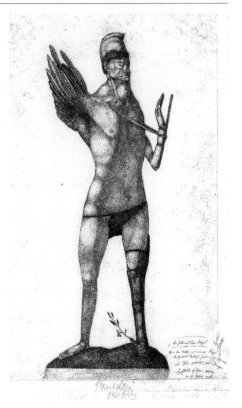

Paul Klee (1879–1940):
The Hero with the Wing (1905)

also delicate and vulnerable — are also the social processes that go along with it. The increasing social complexity leads to an increase in power on the one hand, but on the other, to an ever-increasing interdependence of individuals and peoples.

Paul Klee's hero with one wing symbolizes this dialectical relationship of omnipotence and impotence that characterizes the human condition. »In contrast to divine beings«, Klee's hero »is born with just one angel wing« (Klee 1905, quoted by Friedel 1995, p. 280). He »constantly makes attempts to fly. He breaks his arms and legs in trying, but he

nevertheless perseveres, and remains faithful to his idea«
(ibid.). This masculine hero no doubt embodies the narcissistic »omnipotence-impotence complex« (Richter
1979), from which he cannot escape. There is a striking
contrast between »his monumental, ceremonious attitude«
and the »inherently ruinous condition« in which he really
is (Klee 1905, cited in Friedel 1995, p. 280). This figure is
symbolic of a world destroying its own basis for living and
completing its self-destruction in the illusory faith in its
own grandiosity and power.

We are living during the historic phase of globalization, in
which all parts of the world are connected. All over the world,
resistance is gathering within those parts of the world population who feel disadvantaged and oppressed. The terrorist acts
have been generated from powerlessness, though associated
with mighty sensations of triumph and grandiosity. In terrorism and its opposition, the narcissistic delusions of grandeur
among the powerless, and the smug, grandiose self-image of
the powerful act in disastrous collusion. Since not only America, but also the entire world was struck by the terror attacks,
this applies not merely to the U.S. government; rather, all societies must admit that due to its complexity, our modern civilization is immensely vulnerable. The economically and militarily powerful societies therefore ought to develop a great
interest in what goes on in the minds of the poor, the disadvantaged, and the oppressed. It behooves the powerful and
privileged of the world to use the solidarity and sympathy
shown toward America after the terror attacks from all parts of
the globe as a chance to demonstrate that they are truly interested in a fairer world. September 11 could give the impetus
for supplementing the globalization of world markets with a
globalization of ethics and human sympathy.

Translated by Ingrid G. Lansford, Ph. D.

XENOPHOBIA AND VIOLENCE
AS A FAMILY AND PSYCHOSOCIAL
DISEASE[1]

Prejudice and Enemy Images in Classical
Social Psychology

Prejudice and enemy images are matters studied relatively often in social psychology (cf. Secord & Backman 1974, p. 202 ff.). According to Allport (1954), prejudice is defined as preconceived, negative views and judgments toward a person, a social group, or an object, »based upon a faulty and inflexible generalization« (p. 10). As soon as various characteristic prejudices are combined into a prejudice syndrome, this results in an enemy image. Such enemy images are often directed against racial, national, ethnic or religious groups. Enemy images represent a form of distorted reality perception governed by certain individual and societal interests and needs.

Early research regarded prejudice as the psychological effect of actual conflicts. In his field experiments with American teenagers at summer camps, American social psychologist Mustafa Sherif was able to demonstrate experimentally how prejudices and feelings of hatred may be produced between youth groups by manufacturing conflicts. When the two youth groups were placed in competitive situations, they developed positive solidarity feelings for their in-group and negative stereotypes for their out-

[1] This article was previously published in Piven, Boyd, and Lawton (Eds.). (2002): Jihad and Sacred Vengeance: Psychological Undercurrents of History Volume III. NY (iUniverse), and will also appear in a forthcoming book on domestic violence, edited by David E. Scharff.

group (cf. Secord & Backman 1974). As soon as status differences and scarce resources were added as variables, conflicts were exacerbated.

It is easy to apply Sherif's theory, which has found a place in the history of research as realistic group conflict theory, to the origin and rapid growth of xenophobia in nearly all Western European societies. The high unemployment, the lack of affordable housing, the cuts in social services — all of these phenomena appeared at the same time as the growing hostility against foreigners in the Federal Republic of Germany toward the end of the nineties. They suggest the explanation that xenophobia is caused by competition for scarce but desirable resources. This theory is additionally supported by the fact that xenophobia is most pronounced among population segments in immediate competition and physical proximity to immigrants and asylum-seekers.

In its political application, such theories from social psychology promote the thesis that the German Federal Republic has suffered excessive stress during these times of economic crisis and through the burden of reunification — not just economically, but also emotionally — and that, given these circumstances, the violent excesses against foreigners could only be stopped by drastically limiting their influx (cf. Nicklas 1994, p. 44 ff.).

While the theories of classical social psychology may claim a certain plausibility, their applicability is limited for the following reasons:

1. Enemy images are not necessarily conceived through actual conflicts of interest but rather, it is sufficient for conflicts to exist merely in one's imagination. An extreme example: to quote Theodor W. Adorno, there is even an »anti-Semitism without Jews«.

2. Xenophobia is not a phenomenon limited to the lower third of society. There are also immaterial motives — for instance, religious, ideological, ethnic, psychopathological, etc. — which may lead to the development of prejudices.

3. Classical social psychology has investigated conflicts and oppositions primarily based on actual conflicts of interest, and the accompanying affective and cognitive processes. These theories, however, cannot explain those cases in which there is an excess of aggressive energy, an almost unlimited xenophobia, which goes far beyond a »functional enemy image« that may be useful for developing a feeling of solidarity within a group defining itself in relation to the enemy. As is well known, xenophobia may, in its individual as well as its social manifestations, extend far enough to include the complete destruction of the enemy as well as self-disablement and self-destruction. Here, apparently, an instinctive irrational factor is involved which cannot be explained by the theories mentioned and which calls for more thorough explanations.

Aggression Against Strangers From a Behavioral Viewpoint

Comparative behavioral science may lead to further information. From an ethological view, fear of the stranger, distancing oneself from him, and a latent readiness for aggression against strangers appears, even in humans, to be a »primal phenomenon« developed at an early stage of evolution (cf. Wahl 1994, p. 161). As social beings, humans organize their reproduction in groups. During competition for scarce resources, particularly territories for hunt-

ing and settling, every group of strangers becomes a com-
petitor, opponent, and enemy. In-group egoism and xenophobia appear as anthropological constants.

This ethological attempt at explanation appears valuable insofar as it calls attention to the instinctive-biologi-
cal and natural-animalistic rootedness of humans. The
history of human civilization is relatively brief. In spite of
all civilization, all morality, all technology, and also all
enlightenment, crisis situations always constitute a danger
of regression to pre-civilized, archaic forms of reaction on
the part of the individual and the community as well.
While the higher mammals (barring a few exceptions)
possess an instinctual inhibition against killing members
of their own species, humans are partially free of their instinctive ties to nature (cf. Gehlen 1986). This also includes the freedom, unique to the human species, of being
able to kill fellow humans as well as themselves. Without
social conditioning, civilization, and social integration,
humans are more destructive and self-destructive than any
animal. Nevertheless, ethological theories are limited in
their application for the following reasons:

1. Apart from the image of the evil, frightening stranger,
   there is also the image of the stranger as an attractive,
   interesting, exotic, and enticing being. Ambivalence toward the stranger is deeply rooted in the psyche.
2. Whenever the »primal phenomenon of aggression« is
   mentioned, its opposite, the »primal phenomenon of
   affection« as defined by Schopenhauer and Scheler,
   must also be considered. As Richter (1979) elaborates
   in referring to these authors, the primal phenomenon
   of affection represents »the only original human drive
   in existence which can motivate a reduction of inhu-
   man conditions of oppression« (p. 247) — and, we may
   well add, of xenophobia as well.

3. Culture and civilization developed precisely when the close communities of the family, the kinship group, and the tribe were left behind or evolving into the more complex social structures we call society. Erdheim (1992b) defines culture as that »which develops by dealing with the alien; it represents the product of the transformation through accommodation of the alien« (p. 734).

Fear of Strangers as Viewed by Psychoanalytic Developmental Psychology

Even Freud made theoretical assumptions about the origin of the child's fear of strangers: »A child is frightened of a strange face because he is adjusted to the sight of a familiar and beloved figure — ultimately of his mother. It is his disappointment and longing that are transformed into anxiety« (Freud 1916/17, p. 407).

The well-known »shyness toward strangers« among children has been more closely examined by Rene Spitz (1965), who interprets the so-called »eighth-month anxiety« as a positive sign of maturity, since children are then able to distinguish their mothers from strangers.

As a rule, discussions of shyness toward strangers stress the fear of strangers. With Mario Erdheim (1992a, b), however, I would like to point out its ambivalent character. Shyness with strangers is also »a kind of flirtation, a knock on the door of the unfamiliar« (Erdheim 1992a, p. 21). In their shyness with strangers, children hide in their mothers' arms but continue to peer around the corner, risking a glance at the stranger, only to turn away quickly as soon as the stranger responds to their bid for contact, etc. Shy children thus gain experience by appropriately dosing their affection for strangers. Even babies react to strangers with a »thrill«, with a »fear-desire« (Balint 1959), that is, they hover between fear and curiosity regarding the stranger.

Margaret Mahler (1972) concluded on the basis of her observations that children with a well-developed »basic trust«, as Erikson (1950) defines it, exhibit an exploratory, curious behavior toward strangers. Their developing a fear of strangers depends on the course of earlier interactive experiences. »A child who has been able to develop a sense of security and basic trust does not develop a fear of strangers, but rather a ›customs inspection‹ (Brody & Axelrad 1970), that is, a thorough visual and tactile exploration of an unfamiliar adult« (Mertens 1981, p. 107). »There is a reciprocal relationship between basic trust and fear of strangers« (Bohleber 1994, p. 385).

Michael Rotmann (1978) stresses the importance of the father as »the other« (ibid., p. 1124), as the »third object«, indeed, the representative of the alien world outside, during early child development. The father may become the »significant other« (ibid., p. 1118), the first stranger, who models for the child how the relationship to the mother, as well as a temporary separation from her, may safely take place. The third object permits »early triangulation« (Abelin 1971, quoted by Rotmann 1978), that is, the development of an internal concept of a three-person relationship, giving children the opportunity of integrating their hatred due to frustration by the mother, so that a split between totally »good« and totally »bad« part objects need not occur. As the »attractive third person« (Ermann 1989, p. 265, quoted by Mertens 1992, p. 77), the father offers protection against regression to early mother-child symbiosis on the one hand; on the other, he fulfils an important transitional function for contact with the stranger.

If the father is unavailable in this function, and if the early mother-child relationship is impaired, the child's relationship to the stranger may be characterized by overwhelming fear, a projection of hatred, or by both.

Psychoanalytic family therapy stresses that father and mother become significant objects for the child not only as separate individuals but also as a couple in molding the inner world of the child. The child internalizes the object relationships between himself and his parents as well as those linking father and mother with one another. The self-identity developed by the child is complemented by a social identity, as defined by Mitscherlich (1981). Together, the parent couple and the children develop a »group self« (Erikson 1968, pp. 45–53) and an identity as a family group called »family identity« by Cierpka (1999, p. 91). Whenever the family's group identity is threatened, the need for the family's differentiation from its social environment may receive compensatory special emphasis favoring anxiety toward strangers.

Early child developmental research has called into question several psychoanalytic assumptions concerning early childhood. The old psychoanalytic concept of the infant as an autistic, symbiotic, ambivalent, and passive being has during the past few years been replaced by the concept of — as Martin Dornes (1993) expressed — »the competent infant«, who from the beginning engages in an active interchange with his environment. The assumptions of John Bowlby's »attachment theory«, according to which humans are capable of relationships from birth, and at the same time are beings with an elemental need for attachment, contact and closeness, were hereby confirmed.

Still, the older psychoanalytic theories have not been entirely refuted, but merely relativized. In the first place, phenomena such as passivity, autism, etc. do not occur with each infant, but only as disorders. In the second place, the ambivalence of a child must be regarded as an answer to parental ambivalence. In other words, symbiotic, ambivalent, and autistic tendencies in a child must be regarded as responses to unconscious parental role expectations for the child. This consideration has formed the basis of psychoanalytic family therapy beginning with the early 1960s, since Horst-Eberhard Richter's (1963) book, *Parent, Child, and Neurosis* (*Eltern, Kind und Neurose*); however, it has scarcely been accepted by many psychoanalytic theorists. With respect to the relationship toward strangers, early child developmental research came up with the following differentiations: the attitude toward strangers is typically characterized by three patterns of behavior: children with a secure attachment, children with an insecure, avoiding attachment, and children with an insecure, ambivalent attachment (cf. Dornes 1996, p. 1010). Each of these groups exhibits specific contact behavior toward strangers.

Mario Erdheim (1992 a) deals with the same topic on a more general level. He calls the image of the stranger — analogous to self and object representation — »stranger representation« (p. 21). It offers an alternative, »enabling the child to form an attachment to a person who is not his mother. [This (...)] creates the opportunity of getting something from the stranger which (...) the mother cannot provide« (ibid.). The stranger therefore is a »third object« as defined by Rotmann. On the one hand, it may be stated that fear of strangers increases dependency on familiar objects. On the other hand, it is also true that the more a person's emotional equilibrium depends on the steady presence of one single good object, the greater are that person's fears of strangers. The clinical picture of agoraphobia confirms this.

Agoraphobia and its Political Significance

The symptoms of agoraphobia, that is, fear of public squares, streets, or crowds, may be psychodynamically explained as the fear of losing the attachment figure providing security. Agoraphobia evolves from the conflict between the desires for dependence and independence. Contact with a stranger will unconsciously be sought and dreaded at the same time because it means separation from the mother and might result in her disapproval. For fear of losing the affection of the beloved object, the impulses toward separation and everything related to sexual desires are experienced as »bad«, subsequently repressed, rendered unconscious, and projected upon the unfamiliar. Situations arousing anxiety, such as the street, the public square, the crowd, the stranger, become a screen for the projection of the individual's own repressed impulses.

The stranger representation turns into »a type of house of horrors of the rejected self« (Erdheim 1992b, p. 733). »The advantage is considerable, since the self becomes the good and the unfamiliar becomes the bad«. However, the disadvantage is self-restriction, which results in avoidance of social contact.

Frequently, an anxiety neurosis develops not only in one individual but the entire family becomes involved in the phobic defense strategy so that it withdraws into the controlled environment of a »sanatorium« world. Richter (1970) describes this »sanatorium« as an anxiety-neurotic family type and emphasizes how extraordinarily widespread this is.

One might object that the phobics described here may have a definite fear of strangers; yet, due to their typical denial of aggression and need for harmony, they are hardly in a position to develop hatred toward strangers. This objection is absolutely justified. For anxiety-neurotics, fear of isolation generally leads to an effort to avoid conflict, to establish harmonious relations with their objects, and to reduce contact with the unfamiliar world outside to a minimum.

Typical anxiety-neurotics are distinguished by their particularly compliant adaptation to existing norms and political conditions. Their anxieties force them to sympathize with the traditional — the conservative — and to seek protection by following powerful authority figures. As Richter (1976/1998) puts it, the anxiety-neurotic belongs »to the core group of German fellow travelers« (p. 75). One may thus assume that a large portion of those Germans who took part in National Socialism as fellow travelers, due to their anxiety-neurotic structure, were particularly susceptible to the systematic creation of fear. The National Socialist State systematically created fear and uncertainty and at the same time offered its organizations and leaders as reassuring parent figures. They functioned as superego substitutes, relieving the individual superego and setting it aside.

This attempt at explanation might also contribute to the Goldhagen debate. The questions asked by Goldhagen (1996) were: how could it happen that the overwhelming majority of Germans passively allowed themselves to be integrated and used by the National Socialist regime? Why did hardly anyone refuse to take part in immoral actions (such as shootings) even when such refusal would have been possible without risking life and limb? A partial answer may be found in anxiety-neurotic mechanisms, which operate not only in families but also in groups and organizations. For fear of isolating themselves within the group, individuals submit to the standards and rituals of the group, in particular, the authority of the leader. An additional factor: while during National Socialism many people anxiously withdrew into the supposedly perfect world of the family and refused to pay attention to political events outside, they isolated themselves from the Jews and the Jews from them. The effect of the resulting emotional distance from the Jews was that even many of those who were not at all fanatical Nazi supporters and anti-Semites witnessed the increasing ostracism, persecution, and finally, extermination of the Jews apathetically and without suspicion.

In contrast to Goldhagen, the Polish sociologist Zygmunt Bauman (1993) does not see the central cause of the Holocaust in the long history of European anti-Semitism, but in the process of social distancing from the Jews, which led to a reduction of social responsibility. In the following quotation, it is obvious that Bauman essentially argues from attachment theory:

> »Responsibility, the basic element of moral conduct, results from the proximity of the other. Proximity means responsibility, and responsibility equals proximity. Responsibility disappears as soon as proximity is gone and may even be replaced by resentment if the fellow human is transformed into a stranger. Without social distancing, thousands could not have become murderers, and millions become silent witnesses of the crime.«

Phobic withdrawal from social reality thus brought about apathy toward the fate of Jewish fellow citizens.

While the clinical picture of phobia explains the psychodynamics of the fellow traveler, the mental state of the »silent witness«, it does not explain those of the performing, active perpetrator. The psychodynamics of hatred and violence against strangers call for a different explanation.

Xenophobia as a Narcissistic Disorder

Anxiety is an extremely complex phenomenon. Anxiety may result from many quite different conflicts. If the fear of losing the object does not play the most important part, but rather the fear of being overwhelmed, pursued, tortured, and destroyed by the object, this does not lead to phobic withdrawal but, instead, to other attempts to cope. These consist in distrust of others, projection of one's own hatred onto strangers, narcissistic rage, self-destructive tendencies, and belligerent differentiation from what is outside. Often, the anxiety is linked up with the narcissistic fear of a loss of self-esteem, meaning also the fear of embarrassment and narcissistic insult, often leading to the attempt to keep them in check through narcissistic self-glorification and adherence to dreams of omnipotence. Damaged self-confidence, feelings of inferiority, and self-destructive tendencies are often turned against one's own body. It is treated like an alien object — it becomes a foreign body.

Initially, it may cause surprise that even an individual's body, without which, existence would be impossible, and which therefore forms an integral part of that individual, might be perceived as something alien, as a foreign body. Winnicott (1965/1976) graphically describes how the body must first be appropriated. The self must learn to inhabit the body and feel at home in it (cf. 1992). According to Hirsch (1989/1998), one may psychologically split oneself from one's body and experience it as an object, further acting upon the body as an alien object in imagination and reality (p. vi). Hirsch interprets the syndromes of hypochondria, injuring one's own skin, harming the body through accidents and artificial — that is, deliberately patient-caused — illnesses as manifestations of »destructive acting-out against the body« (p. vi). The body is treated as an external object that is punished by inflicting injury and pain. In order to prevent a threatening fragmentation of the self and keep frightening feelings of hatred against close attachment figures under control, the threat of disintegration is deflected toward the split-off body (cf. Wirth 1996). Frequently, this involves patients who, as children, suffered severe trauma, whom their mothers used as self-objects (cf. Hirsch 1989/1998, p. 97), who had to go through severe deprivation, or who suffered child abuse (cf. Plassmann 1989; Sachsse 1989).

The connection between these clinical syndromes and the phenomenon of xenophobia follows not only from the fact that violent xenophobes, such as German skinheads, frequently act out against their own bodies by such means as tattoos, injuries to the skin with cigarettes, accident-proneness, extreme alcoholic excesses, and the like, but also because the psychodynamic processes are very similar (cf. Auchter 1992; Fischer-Streek 1992). As with AIDS hypochondria, for instance, the existential identity and mortal anxieties manifest themselves through an incorrigible, delusional notion of suffering from a deadly, malignant disease. Similarly, xenophobes are caught up in the fanatical and incorrigible idea that everything »bad« derives solely from the hated stranger (cf. Wirth 1996). They have in common the defense mechanism of splitting. This is the attempt of retaining the »good« object by representing its »bad« parts as completely separate, part-objects. One side is idealized, the other is demonized, and each is projected onto another part-object.

Two Forms of Externalization: Projection and Projective Identification

One may distinguish two types of xenophobia: a fearful and a hate-filled type. The defense mechanism of projection is of central significance in both of them. With xenophobia, the rejected parts are first suppressed and then projected onto the stranger. That is where they are solely perceived from then on, while having been excluded from one's own conscious experience. In order to be able to live relatively free of fear, the phobic need only avoid the frightening stranger.

Xenophobes with a narcissistic disorder present a very different case: they suffer from a particular form of projection: projective identification. Here, the despised portions — in particular, aggressive impulses — are repressed either incompletely or not at all. Thus they remain present in consciousness, and their projection on outside enemies only results in partial relief. It gives rise to the urge to constantly control the object upon whom the aggressive impulses are projected, who is therefore feared (cf. Kernberg 1992). The enemy is not phobically shunned, but instead, a monitoring, aggressive, and persecuting contact is sought. The enemy must be punished or even destroyed. Xenophobes remain consciously identified with their own aggressive impulses even though they have projected them — hence the reason for the term »projective identification«. The complete demonization of the opponent becomes a justification for their own hatred, which is rationalized as mere »counter-aggression«. Typically, projective identification is linked to a distrustful-delusional transformation of reality. The concept of the enemy takes on a paranoid component, becoming an exaggerated fixed idea or ideology which is fanatically defended against all doubters. Finally, a total fixation on the fight against the pursuer develops, including putting oneself at risk rashly (Richter 1978/1996, p. 121 ff.), as is also known from political conflicts.

The following two case narratives represent an attempt to contribute to a better understanding of the psychodynamics of xenophobia.

Ivo's Case

Ivo, a 24 year-old, tall mathematics student, was suffering from three disorders:

1. A severe obsessive-compulsive neurosis which had occurred for the first time at age six when his mother became ill with a stomach and intestinal flu and he was afraid he would lose her. He reported that in the time following this incident, he had begun to observe extreme cleanliness, worry about cancer, and developed a fear of being poisoned by food. His compulsive acts consisted of making sure doors and windows were locked, »sniffing« his fingers, and observing certain rituals while working. The symptoms had supposedly increased about a year earlier, ever since he had neared the completion of his mathematical studies.

2. In tandem with the compulsive symptomatology a severe paranoia had developed. The patient had only had one close friend in his entire life but finally lost him through quarreling. Having been constantly laughed at and teased for being unathletic in school, Ivo had adopted an outsider role. He accounted for his social isolation with a paranoid ideology by ascribing the causes to society and substantiating this by means of far-fetched rationalizations: he was, after all, a »loner

and individualist«, and because of this automatically came into conflict with the conformist »men of the crowd«, among whom he also included his father. Instead of associating with people his own age, Ivo conducted chemical experiments at home and built bombs. His grades — except in sports — had always been excellent. His parents idealized him as a scientific genius, and he too saw himself in the role of the unrecognized genius.

3. Another disorder consisted of a perversion, namely, pedophilic inclinations, in which the patient partly indulged in his imagination, but also by making social contact with children. So far, no manifestly pedophilic contact had occurred. He experienced his pedophilic longings and fantasies, which exclusively involved pre-pubescent girls, as ego-syntonic and vehemently defended them against any arguments.

The patient was an only child and had very close ties to his mother. His father had not wanted children and indeed soon disappointedly rejected the clumsy, awkward, mother-fixated son. Father and son avoided one another and only communicated through the mother. Ivo said of his father, »My father is pretty superficial. I don't consider him very intelligent either. He always interrupts when I'm talking to my mother. My father has no idea at all what is going on inside me.« The father's opinion of the son: »He wasn't much use even as a little kid. He didn't want to play ball or get involved in any sport at all. He was simply difficult all the time and was tied to his mother's apron strings. I really have given up on him.«

The father exhibited a compulsive character structure and aroused feelings of disgust in his son when he »flicks his dried snot all over our apartment«. He taught biology, had also grown up as an only child, and had lost his father in the war at an early age. Until late adolescence he had slept in the same room with his mother.

Ivo's mother was suffering from cardiac-neurotic symptoms, but counterphobically dismissed them. She had grown up with her mother and grandmother, »without a man in the family«. Her own mother was extremely fearful, and she had always had the job of protecting her, for instance, from geese. Ivo's mother grew up in Communist East Germany under very modest circumstances, and had been quite successful as a gymnastic performer and subsequently as a trainer.

Ivo had been sleeping in the marital bed next to his mother since he was ten years old. His father slept in his son's room. Only after several years of family therapy did they begin to understand their feelings, experience some transformation, and change their sleeping arrangements. The nearly complete absence of feelings of embarrassment among all family members was striking.

This case is relevant to our topic insofar as the parents embraced a militant and fanatically expressed anti-Semitism. They denied the Holocaust, spoke hatefully of foreigners and asylum-seekers, and sympathized with political parties on the right. In this aspect, the mother was the most dominant and the most fanatical, but the father also became animated on this topic and argued very heatedly. He also articulated such slogans at school, sometimes meeting with agreement, sometimes with vigorous resistance. He avoided the »environmentalist screwballs« among his colleagues altogether. The patient himself was less committed regarding these issues, but whenever I asked for his opinion, he uncritically repeated everything his mother had drummed into him. On the other hand, he had accepted his mother's values not merely on this, but practically all matters concerning the outside world.

Whenever I made a cautious attempt to question the family's anti-Semitism and xenophobia, I came up against a wall of incomprehension and disapproval. Dealing with this topic required a delicate balance. On the one hand I did not want to avoid the topic altogether, because I considered the anti-Semitism and xenophobia important symptomatic components of the pathological family system, but on the other hand, I sensed the danger of getting into a confrontational discussion, which would only end in breaking off the therapy. By Richter's (1970) definition from the viewpoint of family diagnosis, this involved a »paranoid fortress family« that had formed a tight unit against an outside world felt to be hostile and harassing (p. 90 ff.).

Ivo's self-image was characterized by the idea of being a poor, innocent victim who was persecuted, humiliated and devalued on all sides for his pedophilic inclinations. He could get worked into truly hateful tirades when talking of politicians who wanted to increase punishment for the sexual abuse of children. His particular enemy was the Minister of Justice. By the way, Ivo explicitly distanced himself from sexual violence and repeatedly stressed that what mattered to him was for the little girls to give him their love voluntarily. The patient considered himself a martyr who must suffer for a good cause, the sexual liberation of the child. He appeared to derive masochistic enjoyment from feeling so unappreciated. His masochistic acting out included a fantasy of omnipotence, a masochistic triumph derived from the dream of being indispensable to the sadistic agent (manifestly, the politicians the patient opposed, subconsciously, his father), and through his masochistic availability, becoming a rescuer to this sadistic oppressor and therefore superior and more powerful than he. At the same time, this political struggle for the rights of children gave him a partial sense of identity. People took note of him now; he no longer was anonymous, even though they rejected, condemned, and despised him for his opinions. Besides, their vehement accusations relieved him from moral self-recrimination for his incestuous and perverted fantasies. At the same time, this supposed misjudgment of him was his justification for venting hatred and aggression. At last he had found a legitimate way of redirecting his self-hatred outside. It was not the case that he was prejudiced, but that others hated him because they were prejudiced. While Ivo fired his barrage of hatred at the politicians, he felt big and superior, and one could actually notice his working himself into a hypomanic state which was clearly designed to ward off his subliminal, depressive feelings of inferiority. The contempt and rejection Ivo met with confirmed his delusional feeling of grandiosity and superiority. The patient attempted to restore his injured feelings of self-worth through reactive hatred. In his destructive daydreams he worked himself up into the idea of destroying the entire world with a giant atomic bomb.

The psychodynamic, or family dynamic, was the following: the patient had an intense, incestuously charged relationship with his mother. On the one hand he felt like an Oedipal winner as a science genius who had outdone his father, whose place near the mother he had captured. On the other hand, he felt diminished, supervised, castrated, and infantilized by his mother. His obsessive neurosis served as protection from incest, and thus as protection from canceling all limits and rules and entering the psychotic state. The obsessions gave structure to this unstructured family that denied the distinction between generations.

The second protective barrier against incest was his pedophilia. Through his choice of objects, the patient avoided making his mother jealous. In fact, his mother supported his pedophilic interests in arranging for him to meet little girls in her gym class. Ivo could only imagine a sexual partner of childlike innocence and purity because he recoiled from the genitals of an adult woman. Indeed, his mother used to change her sanitary napkin in front of little Ivo. While Chasseguet-Smirgel (1975) writes, »If the sight of the female genital organs is so ›traumatic,‹ it is because it confronts the young male with his inadequacy, because it forces him to recognize his oedipal defeat« (p. 15 f), Ivo's case instead suggests that the sight of the female genitals in itself has no traumatizing effect, but rather, the surrounding relationship dynamics involved.

Family dynamics philosophy could answer Freud's (1927) question why »the fright of castration at the sight of the female genital« which »probably no male human being is spared« makes »some people become homosexual as a consequence of that impression, while others fend it off by creating a fetish, and the great majority surmount it« (p. 154). This way, the unconscious parental role assignments for the child have a »traumatizing« effect. Chasseguet-Smirgel (1975) expresses this insight somewhat more cautiously: »Perhaps one might claim that those who become perverts are those who, often with their mothers' encouragement, could not reconcile themselves to giving up the illusion of being able to make a satisfying partner for her« (p. 16).

On a pre-Oedipal level Ivo was trying to ward off his feelings of hatred and narcissistic fury toward his mother, whom he experienced as seductive and overwhelming, but also frustrating, through idealization and sexualization (cf. Becker 1996, p. 233; Stoller 1979). Ivo would fall in love with little girls, who presented an embodiment of himself and to whom he wanted to give the considerate love his mother had denied him (cf. Berner 1996, p. 1044; Fenichel 1931). He denied the destructive aspects of pedophilia which surfaced split off in his fantasies of bomb production and thinking in terms of an enemy image.

Because of her narcissistic personality structure, his mother was hardly able to experience insight, intense emotion, recognition of guilt, or even feelings of shame, and remained caught up in denial, rationalization, and projective assignment of guilt. The mother had abused her son narcissistically and, in a certain sense, also sexually. The son's pedophilia was actually an escape from incest. In analogy with Ferenczi's »Confusion of Tongues Between Adults and the Child« (1933), the patient became mixed up, confusing ideas of love in reaction to the traumatizing, sexually narcissistic exploitation by the mother. This also included neglect of his body, his clothing, and his appearance. He always stressed that all of this was insignificant to him. He had, so to speak, let his mother have his body, and it was she who — as was easy to see — picked out his clothes. He looked as obedient and proper as a first-grade boy in the 1950s. The confusion within him also made him doubt his perception of reality. It was a sign of the weakening of his reality testing caused by his trauma. It happened over and over that he would literally look to his mother for reassurance that his opinion on a matter had her confirmation, support, and approval. When talking during the therapy session, he sometimes suddenly stopped, afraid, and looked at his mother questioningly. She, however, had learned very quickly from therapy that I had a critical attitude toward her manipulation and infiltration of her son. She maintained silence and laughed when her son gave her an uncertain and questioning look. In this way, the patient's doubts about his own perception and above all, the validity of his affects, were further increased, and his inability to perform a reality check in certain areas grew to a pseudo-debility. With regard to social contacts, the patient was at the baby stage. He did not seem to be viable without his mother. In particular, due to his mother's sudden shifts between emotional closeness and cool rejection, he was subjected to a kind of brainwashing so that he remained in the dark about which were his own or his mother's needs. The patient had to perceive his mother's behavior as a constant attack on his experience of reality as the intrusion of her needs into his identity represented a steady violation of boundaries. Again and again, it was difficult for him to distinguish his own needs from those of his mother, in particular because the over-stimulation aroused his own (yet, unknown) needs. As far as that went, it was a matter of blurring the borders between self and object, i. e. an attack on his basic feeling of identity, so that he depended on his mother's presence even during that time in order to maintain a feeling of completeness and the ability to survive in social life at all. Since the father had failed completely as a »saving third person«, the family revolved around the mother-son incest. As often occurs in cases of abuse, paradoxically it was the perpetrator who was most readily identified as a good parent figure because the child, in his identification with the aggressor, »tries to save himself by trying to maintain the relationship vital to him by regarding himself as the cause of the violence and the evil, and assigning the blame to himself« (Hirsch 1996, p. 35).

The lack of modesty among all family members was striking. Thus the mother, when I asked her, reported that as a matter of course she always undressed completely in front of her son. »That's no big deal, we are all members of the same family,« she told me so provocatively that I was embarrassed. I would frequently be affected by the countertransferential feeling of embarrassment, and I gradually became aware that the family induced the feeling of embarrassment within me because it needed to fend off its own embarrassment. Ivo had transformed the sense of inferiority, insecurity, and embarrassment he must have felt as a child taunted by his classmates for being a mama's boy into a provocative display of his perverted sexuality in order to embarrass the other person.

This concludes the case narrative. For comparison, another case shall be presented as an example: that of the radical rightist violent skinhead Max. A comparison between Ivo and Max should be interesting from a methodological viewpoint as well. It is a comparison — from a superficial angle — between two extremely different personality types who seem to resemble one another only in one way, i. e. their highly developed xenophobia. On the one hand, there is the awkward and effeminate Ivo, who clings to his mother in anxious infantilism and has grown up in a middle-class family, an unathletic dreamer, a strict non-drinker, and militant non-smoker. On the other, we have the provocative ugliness of a skinhead with his brute physicality, his tattoos, his bald head and combat boots, yelling, smoking, and drinking beer. Two people could hardly be more different. But why do they have the phenomenon of xenophobia in common? In the two cases, is xenophobia based on similar causes, or on entirely different causes and mechanisms?

Max the Skinhead

Eighteen-year-old Max was a member of a skinhead gang of about nine members. Within the scope of a research project on youthful subcultures, I made contact with him through the social worker in charge of his apartment-sharing group. Max immediately declared himself willing to meet with my colleague Monika Reinitz and me. He arrived on time and in his complete skinhead outfit. Proudly, he showed us his most important status symbol, his Doc Marten's boots, and explained to us their difference from other types of boots. He tried to hide his initial insecurity by reeling off anecdotes and mottos in staccato delivery. As for contents, his conversation began quite stereotypically, as did almost all of our interviews with skinheads: Max complained about the unwarranted rejection and prejudice he had to put up with from other people again and again. They assumed he was brutal, violent, and a Nazi. But all of that, he said, was nothing but prejudice.

We got the feeling that Max wanted to put us to the test as to whether we too would reject and condemn him. Besides, the circumstance of his outsider role was of such fundamental significance to his identity that it became a direct or indirect topic of conversation during every contact with non-skinheads.

While Max complained about his outsider role at first, it became clear later on that his identity was at the same time reinforced by the rejection he constantly experienced: »When several skinheads walk down the street together, people make room. They're scared of us. That somehow builds you up. When I still ran around looking normal, and I would put my legs up on the seat of the bus, I would get snapped at. If I do this now as a skinhead, people leave me alone. You are really the same guy, but as a skin, you get bigger, and the others react to you differently.«

Max strongly disassociated himself from the punks he used to sympathize with: One could only support their mottos »null bock« (not turned on) and »no future« »if one is way at the bottom. I have never felt like the lowest of the low, I have never been that far down. When I had my null bock trip, I wound up in the slammer. That built me back up. After that, I became a skinhead.«

In this brief passage, on the one hand Max denied having felt far down and »like the lowest of the low«, but on the other, he confessed that this has been the case after all: When he had his »null bock trip«, he wound up in the slammer. Max was searching for firm, supporting structures and »paternal« authority, apparently finding this in the institution of the prison, which he did not perceive as a punishment« but where he even felt »built up«. He made an immediate connection between prison and the skinhead group in which he apparently found similar support. Max stressed the strong group solidarity of the skinheads. »That the group sticks together is the most important thing to me. When someone is in trouble, all the others come up right away, and then watch out.« He also liked about the skinheads »that we don't just hang around like the punks and drink but also do something, like, go to soccer games and beat up squatters.«

When we asked him about his family, the biographical background responsible for his feeling of being the lowest of the low was revealed: Max had never come to know his father. His dad left the family shortly after Max's birth and never made support payments. Soon his mother could no longer manage Max. He was placed with a foster family and afterward, in a children's home. Then his mother repeatedly got him back. This never worked out for long, and so he went back and forth between the children's home and his mother for several years. By the time of the interview he had practically no contact with her. He only rarely went to L. to visit her.

As for his relationships with women, Max said that the skinheads did not think much of women. They were regarded as »chewing gum, as cigarette paper, as toilet paper, used and then tossed out.« Still, in answer to the question of whether he had ever been in love, he spoke of a houseparent who was ten years older with whom he had remained in touch for several years. Whenever he felt bad, he could always call her up, even in the middle of the night. »After my first fight I called her up and wound up crying my eyes out,« although just before that he had been bragging to his friends about what a hero he was. Max wanted to impress the houseparent but he was afraid that this relationship might also end if he made too much mischief. Max appeared visibly moved when he talked of this, but then wanted to leave this topic and return to the skinheads.

He said that most of the skinheads were ultra-rightists. He himself no longer wanted any part in Nazi slogans. He no longer wanted to submit to the pressure of the group. Yet the skinheads were not real Nazis at all, he said, because they did not have much patience with the recruiting attempts of a Nazi organization. On the other hand, he too could endorse the slogan »I take pride in being a German!« — »That's totally normal and has nothing to do with Fascism. I am exercising the same right as young people from other nations.« When asked about the xenophobia of the skinheads, Max squirmed. While he admitted that many skinheads hated the Turks for taking jobs away from Germans, he explicitly distanced himself from any hostility toward foreigners. We had the impression that during the entire conversation, Max was trying to convey to us that he did not fit the negative image of the violent, ultra-rightist skinheads. Even Max was, apparently, subject to the social pressure exerted by the relatively intimate conditions of the interview. The tendency to answer in accordance with »what's socially desirable« was, incidentally, also evident with other skinheads, above all, in one-on-one interviews. This shows that skinheads have a desire for social acceptance and that it is also expressed in their personal contacts even though in their public behavior, they appear to be only interested in provoking disapproval.

Toward the end, our conversation took a surprising turn. Max declared that his chief enemies were not foreigners but the people of the Vogelsberg region. When we asked him, surprised, whether he really considered everyone living in the Vogelsberg region his enemy, Max let loose a torrent of words about »the stupidity of the peasants of Vogelsberg«, whom he called »assholes, scum of the nation« and »the Jews of today ... whose turn it would be if Hitler were alive«. Max worked himself up into a real fury. He told us about a raid he had recently undertaken to L. with his skinhead group in order to »take apart a disco« there. It had resulted in several wounded, and he himself could only be stopped by a massive deployment of police.

When he mentioned the town of L., it suddenly hit us: Max was driving to the town where his mother lived, the place where — as it turned out — he was born, in order to demolish everything and vent all of his pent-up hatred. As soon as we cautiously hinted at this connection, Max started to feel uncomfortable. He began to object and refused to talk about the subject any further, saying that if he did, there was a risk that we too would start hating the people in the Vogelsberg region. We understood that Max's fear of reliving the hurts received in childhood and the resulting feelings of hatred was so great that he was afraid they might overwhelm both him and us. We therefore did not press him any further. The next appointment with Max did not take place because he joined the German army shortly afterwards, and we lost contact with him.

Max's basic attitude toward life was marked by the many deep disappointments and injuries he had experienced as a child abandoned and given away by father and mother. To give other people affection and friendship, even to love and trust them, were modes of experience Max regarded as overwhelming risks because the early disappointment, pain, and humiliation of his childhood might be repeated. All his effort went toward avoiding this. His narcissistic counter-ideals of coldness, contempt of human ideals, lack of empathy, dehumanization of his adversary, and gnawing resentment against all that seemed to him a sign of weakness, helplessness and softness, served that goal.

This also showed in his split concept of women. Max perceived women as either »sacred mothers« or »contemptible whores«. Such a view was the result of a psychic process in which both his own identity and his image of other people was split into absolutely good and absolutely bad parts. The split developed as a defense against equally intense feelings of hatred and of being destroyed or abandoned, originating from his poor relationship with his mother. The split characterized not only Max's image of women but also his perception of the world in general. His paranoia-charged aggression surfaced in hatred for all that was foreign, and in resentment against interchangeable victims. On the other hand, his »pride in being a German« appeared as a feeble attempt to pit against his self-hatred something positive he could idealize. He used the common ultra-rightist motto »I take pride in being a German« as an antidote to the hurtful realization that he had truly felt treated like »the lowest of the low« all his life. His contempt for humanity derived from his auto-biographical experience of always being the outcast, the disadvantaged, cheated, and deceived. His self-contempt, self-hatred, and self-destructive impulses and actions corresponded to the contempt others had for him. One part of Max remained identified with his traumatizing mother, whom he experienced as sadistic and mean. His sadistic part-identity inflicted upon others (and on him-self) the viciousness he himself once had to endure, while his despised masochistic part-identity identified with the victim. By idealizing power and terror derived from contempt for humanity, he tried to reverse the traumatization he had suffered in the past: he now wished to be as strong and frightening as he had once perceived his dreaded »bad« mother to be, but thereby again and again inevitably placed himself in the role of the persecuted victim.

A Comparison of the Two Cases

Several remarkable parallels appear in these two cases.

1. With both men, the feeling of being victims and therefore always being treated unfairly constitutes their identity. They believe that others consider them an incar-nation of evil and identify with the victim role because this enables them to turn the defeat, shame, and fear they have passively suffered into action. Instead of suffering fear themselves, they instil fear and terror in others. Their internal conflict is converted back into an external conflict. Functioning as an enemy image for others legitimizes the

retention of their own enemy image. Their negative self-image and enemy image are closely linked. This is the particular characteristic of projective identification. Once one has had the traumatizing experience of being pushed into the role of the scapegoat, one may see a way out by looking for an enemy and scapegoat of one's own on whom to project one's rejected parts, and whom one persecutes and humiliates. The dynamics of enemy images call for continuous propagation.

2. Both of these young people believe that society has inflicted great injustice on them. They are therefore conscious that a principle of justice exists and that it has been grievously violated. Leon Wurmser (1987) considers this an important criterion for the development of enemy images and resentments. With xenophobia, revenge serves as compensatory justice for a putative — yet, frequently also actual — injustice. The feeling of having been dealt with unjustly represents a basic motive for xenophobia. This could be one of the reasons why xenophobia is a greater problem in former Communist East Germany than in West Germany.

3. With both protagonists, a defense against feelings of shame through conversion from passivity to activity plays a central role. Ivo converts his tormenting feelings of inferiority and shame into the deliberate flaunting of his obscenity and perversity. He is no longer the small, insecure boy exposed to the jokes and contemptuous glances of others but a professed pederast, embarrassing the listener by his sexual confessions.

This is similar with Max: his ugliness, provocatively displayed, forces others to avert their eyes in fear and embarrassment, »allowing the former victim of shaming and ugliness to become the perpetrator. Subjective feelings of powerlessness and weakness are turned into belligerent strength, arousing fear in others. The scornful grin often to be observed with skinheads expresses this ›victory‹« (Hilgers 1996, p. 168). Shame, rage, and delusions of grandeur are the basic manifestations of a disturbed narcissistic equilibrium. Narcissistic insults may lead to shameful retreat, grandiose fantasies, or narcissistic rage. The latter is characterized by a lust for revenge and unbounded obsession and leads to the paranoid development of enemy images. The narcissistic rage serves the »archaic grandiose self« (Kohut 1971), based on the unconditional availability of the approving and reflecting function of an admiring self-object or on the ever-present opportunity for fusion with an »idealized self-object« (Kohut 1971). Despite their differences, the narcissistic fury of the skinheads and that of Ivo have certain traits in common because both of them are rooted within the matrix of a narcissistic world view. Neither of them can muster the slightest bit of understanding for those who insult them. Both of them react with an irreconcilable fury as soon as they lose control over the mirroring self-object. Thus, Ivo was often beside himself with rage when his mother would not answer his questions or his father would not understand what he wanted. With the skinheads, too, it only takes seemingly minor provocations — for instance someone who looks different from how they think he should — to trigger an outburst of narcissistic fury.

In dealing with violence-prone young people, civic authorities are confronted with a dilemma: If they use all their power in an attempt to force compliance with law and order, they humiliate the adolescents, which leads to further escalation of violence because the young people will seek to restore their lost honor by renewed violence. However, if the police seem to signal their latent consent or weakness by tolerating violent excesses, the adolescents will break out in a disappointed rage over the weakness of authority. This means that for these specific conflicts, rules must be established which respect the dignity of the participants. There must be limits, but without humiliation of the other party.

4. In both cases, the manifest enemy images have only taken over a substitute function for a hatred whose affective roots go deeper. One might suspect that the real hatred was for the »bad mother«, who was smothering in Ivo's case, and in Max's case, negligent. There is much to favor this interpretation. However, is that really the entire story? In both cases there are additional enemy images. Max fights with the police. Ivo's favorite enemy is the Minister of Justice. Both enemy images are easy to identify as paternal authority figures. With Ivo as with Max, the father was missing as a »saving third person«. The child was abandoned to the frustrating mother without protection. Early triangulation did not take place. For that reason no integration of good and bad introjections occurred. Since both young men had to do without the presence of a father, they subconsciously long for structuring father figures to come up against. Max's violent rampages as well as Ivo's sexual provocations are always designed to challenge societal authority into a reaction that will impose limits. Both young men are characterized by a deep longing for a father (cf. Aigner 2001) which manifests itself in the provocation of societal (paternal) authorities, as well as by a masochistic, somewhat passively homosexual need for punishment.

5. With Ivo just as with Max, the enemy image their respective attachment group has selected — which I call the collective enemy image — conceals another, quite personal enemy image — which I call the private enemy image — of greater autobiographical significance. The

private hatred appears even more irrational and eccentric than the collective hatred. It pushes the individual into the role of the outsider, the lunatic, since hardly anyone shares the private enemy image. The person who wishes to have his feelings of hatred accepted within a group will therefore shift his hatred to an object that others, too, have chosen as an enemy image. On the one hand, collective enemy images derive their affective energy in part from individual pathologies. On the other hand, individuals find relief from the pressure of psychological conflict by letting their affects merge into the collective enemy image. Apparently, enemy images are easily interchangeable. Freud's remarks that religion constitutes a collective neurosis may be applied to the enemy image. Enemy images are collective narcissistic disorders.

Together with Georges Devereux (1978, 1980), one could also make a distinction between an idiosyncratic and an ethnic emotional disorder. The idiosyncratic disorder develops due to very specific circumstances in the life of an individual. On the other hand, an ethnic disorder involves not just separate individuals but a large number of the members of a collective. This corresponds to the »ethnic unconscious« which constitutes that part of the unconscious the individual shares with the majority of the members of the culture (1980, p. 6). While the ethnic unconscious arises from what the culture teaches to suppress, the »idiosyncratic unconscious« is mainly based on defensive familial constellations (p. 7). »Culture itself provides the individual with directives for the misuse of cultural material« (p. 29), so-called »patterns of misconduct«, allowing deviant behavior in a socially acceptable manner. The motto might be: »Don't do it, but if you do, go about it in this manner« (ibid.).

6. Patients who structure their early psychosomatic disorder as an illness and thus seek to control it, as a rule still have close family contact, usually to their family of origin, but sometimes also to partners. Their illness includes a social function and meaning in this closer social, mostly familial context. Self-injuries and suicide attempts have high interactional significance and elicit intense emotional actions and reactions (cf. Sachsse 1989, p. 104). I suspect that with clinical syndromes during the early mother-child dyad, the attachment mode is dominant, while among the xenophobes, an expulsion mode is more likely to dominate. Xenophobes and violent individuals therefore do not seek a familial context but rather, a peer group context where they can find support, recognition, acceptance, and the company of like-minded people with whom they may organize their narcissistic disorder and act it out. Collective ideologies and enemy images are more likely to be found in groups, while a private ideology is more prevalent in families.

7. As a counterpart of their negative enemy image, both young men have built up an ideal image which is exaggerated, contradictory and, by the definition of Janine Chasseguet-Smirgel (1975, 1986), »false«: Ivo idealizes the purity, tenderness, and innocence of pedophilic love. The »falseness« of this idealization lies in the denial of sexual coercion inherent in pedophilia.

Max, on the other hand, has made the German nation his ideal. He stresses his »pride in being German«. In »Phantasm of the Nation« (»Phantasma der Nation«, Bohleber 1992), the unconscious wish for »pre-ambivalent fusion with an idealized object is fulfilled« (p. 689). Concepts such as people, nation, and race »invite participation in something large, exalted, and powerful, transcending one's own existence and promising recognition without regard to social position« (Neckel 1991, p. 168). Persons who, because of a narcissistic insult, suffer from feelings of powerlessness, of injustice, and of their own worthlessness, are particularly dependent on this type of self-affirmation and recognition. This has also been shown by the research of Heitmeyer (1992) and associates with (predominantly male) young people from socio-economically depressed areas who, as so-called »victims of modernization«, are particularly vulnerable to rightist extremism. »People, nation and race are categories of evaluation of the self and others which may apply even when all other categories — money, power, knowledge, and prestige [and satisfying personal relationships] — have already failed« (ibid., p. 169), or are expected to fail. For those who feel inferior, these serve as identity props, coming all the more prominently to the fore, the fewer other sources of recognition appear to be available.

> »Participation in the great, superior collective of a particular people promises transcendence of the narrowness and limitation of one's own existence. The collective symbol radiates sublimely despite the self-perceived lowliness of one's own circumstances, indeed, increasing in fascination when one's individual circumstances are becoming ever more depressing.« (ibid., p. 161)

The demonstrative pride in being a German and differentiation from foreigners who are considered inferior serves to shore up their own injured self-confidence.

Final Comments

My attempt to interpret xenophobia and violence as symptoms of a psychosocial disease is based on a specific definition of disease (cf. Auchter 1992). The mania of xenophobia has an unconscious purpose, fulfilling a psychological and social function. With respect to this opinion I shall refer to physicist and philosopher Carl Friedrich von Weizsäcker (1967), to whose lecture »Belligerence as a Mental Disease« (»Friedlosigkeit als seelische Krankheit«) my title alludes. By explicitly calling it a »disease«, I wished to make plain that it involves neither stupidity nor innate malice. This is the exact reason why xenophobia will not be overcome through either lectures or condemnation. It requires different procedures that might be called therapy, healing, communication, and perhaps also enlightenment in an empathic sense.

Translated by Ingrid G. Lansford, Ph. D.

Emigration, Biography and Psychoanalysis: Jewish Psychoanalysts who Emigrated to the United States of America

Hans-Jürgen Wirth and Trin Haland-Wirth

Psychoanalysis and Emigration

On the one hand, psychoanalysis is an instrument which allows us to analyze the fate and the biography of emigrants and their psychodynamics. On the other hand, psychoanalysis, as an institution and a large number of its early representatives, has painfully suffered from the fate of emigration. Therefore, it is odd that even decades after World War II only a few articles and books have been published on this topic (cf. Grinberg & Grinberg 1984; Timms & Segal 1988; Stadler 1988, p. 212–250; Akhtar 1999; Rodewig 2000; Bell et al. 2002). Even in the field of psychoanalytic Holocaust research, only a few have given their undivided attention to emigration (cf. Bergmann et al. 1982). Only since psychotherapeutic work with extremely traumatized victims of torture, persecution, violence and war was noticed, have more and more psychoanalytic publications about emigration been written (cf. Bell et al. 2002; Haubl et al. 2003; Eckart & Seidler, in press).

Even Sigmund Freud and his mostly Jewish followers were banished not only from their city of origin Vienna and from all of Austria and Germany, but also from Hungary, Czechoslovakia, Italy, France and Belgium. They were banished everywhere the National Socialists came into power. Freud's writings were burned and psychoanalytic institutions were destroyed or controlled by the Nazis — as in the case of the Göring Institute in Berlin (cf. Lockot 2003).

It is significant that many psychoanalysts — although not all of them (cf. Mühlleitner 1992; Hermanns 2001; Kaufhold 2003 a, p. 64) — were able to escape in time before the Holocaust began. One could come up with the hypothesis that this had something to do with the fact that from the very beginning psychoanalysts had already been excluded from society and therefore were very alert. "As Freud (1925) pointed out, it was not only during its early stages that psychoanalysis "unleashed a storm of indignant rejection" (ibid., p. 101). Rather, one has to be aware that society is "in opposition" to psychoanalysis because it has evoked "resistances different from merely intellectual ones", namely, "powerful affective forces" (ibid., p. 104). Psychoanalysis was attacked because it placed a mirror on society which showed everyone how society's double standard causes the development of psychic disorders. Large parts of society had the feeling that especially the discovery of the infantile sexuality was a break of taboo. Therefore, Freud's theories and his new research methods (which were treatment methods at the same time) were rejected and said to be unscientific and speculative because they did not fulfill the natural scientific ideal of methods.

The psychoanalytic community developed into an open or latent hostile environment. The identity of the psychoanalysts as a group was determined by the awareness of being an outsider. From the beginning, psychoanalysis had to deal with rejection, hostility, even persecution by society. All psychoanalysts — especially Freud himself — went through these experiences and analyzed them with the help of the psychoanalytic method as a type of resistance. The widespread anti-Semitism and Freud's Jewishness, which he »never wanted to hide« (ibid., p. 110), played a central role in it. It was quite clear to Freud from the beginning and was even a motive for him to choose one of the few non-Jewish psychoanalysts, the »Teuton« Carl Gustav Jung, as Freud wrote in a letter to Ferenczi (quoted by Gay 1987, p. 231), as president of the International Psychoanalytic Association (IPA).

The community of psychoanalysts was therefore more sensitive to the possibility of persecution than other Jewish professional groups, in which many of them assimilated completely. But were the psychoanalysts really protected by their outsider identity from the illusion of hope that the Nazis would not attack them? Bernd Nitzschke pointed out that the opposite was the case: »The group of psychoanalysts was — at least concerning their manifest behavior— extremely ›illusionary‹ and tried to hold on to practicing politics of ›un‹-political attitudes — so to speak: of adaptation — until the bitter end. Wilhelm Reich (cf. Fallend & Nitzschke 2002) in particular protested unsuccessfully against this« (Nitzschke 2003). Many psychoanalysts managed to escape because until 1938, the main goal of the Nazis was to force the Jews to emigrate. At the beginning of the war, they closed the borders and explained their main goal: the annihilation of all Jews.

But »in spite of the relative adaptation and the depoliticized attitude against the Austro Faschism, the members of Viennese Psychoanalytic Association were hit by political reaction« (cf. Mühlleitner, Reichmayr 2003, p. 74), and after 1933 the first wave of emigration started in Germany and then in 1934 in Austria. Between 1933 and 1938, a total of 28 Viennese psychoanalysts who were members of the Viennese Psychoanalytic Association left the country (ibid.). For example, »Siegfried Bernfeld, who was a well-known socialist and an excellent psychoanalytic speaker, went to France and then fled to London in 1937 and from there to San Francisco. Edith Buxbaum, a Social Democrat and a high school teacher, was arrested in 1935 and left Austria in 1937 and went to the USA. In 1934 and 1935, respectively, Felix and Helene Deutsch emigrated to Boston« (ibid.). The reaction of those psychoanalysts who at the time decided not to emigrate was conflicting: In a letter to her friend Lou Andreas-Salomé, Anna Freud wrote that she was very disappointed Helene Deutsch emigrated: »It really hurt my feelings that she simply left us« (quoted by Mühlleitner & Reichmayr 2003, p. 72). Evidently the Viennese psychoanalysts were profoundly split concerning the necessity of emigration, respectively the necessity to hold out in Vienna.

In every case, psychoanalysts had many international contacts at their disposal in comparison to most of the other Jewish professional groups. If they decided to emigrate, those contacts would be very helpful. For instance, the immigration to America depended on whether the immigrant found an American citizen who was willing to sign a document stating he would financially support the immigrant in case of emergency. No immigrant should ever be a burden on the country. This so-called »affidavit« was the desired ticket to the United States. The fact that many Americans had gone to Vienna in the twenties in order to receive psychoanalytic training turned out to be very beneficial for the emigrants. The Americans came to Vienna to receive psychoanalytic training from first-hand psychoanalysts. Besides that, many professionals who were not medical doctors and worked in the pedagogical and social fields were not allowed to take part in the psychoanalytic training in America. Therefore, they were forced to go to Vienna, where they could become »lay analysts« (cf. Kaufhold 2003 a, p. 40). Many of them joined Anna Freud's Viennese pedagogical group and others founded therapeutic schools and kindergartens. Hereby the group of psychoanalysts, the young analysts in training and the Americans built up a close relationship. They translated Freud's and other analysts' writings into English, which helped them work together in Austria and later in the US. A few analysts even taught English to the Viennese, which helped them later on when they emigrated. Since the Americans were only guests in Austria and not directly affected, some of them used their position and their contacts to help the Viennese leave the country. A few of these Americans were even involved in the illegal underground battle and provided them with affidavits and fake passports, money, and hid analysts from the Nazis.

One of the most daring people was the American psychoanalyst Muriel Gardiner. In 1935 she began »to help — together with her future husband, Joseph Buttinger, chief (Obmann) of the Revolutionary Socialists — many endangered socialists leave Austria. Gardiner was an American psychoanalyst who studied medicine in Vienna and received her psychoanalytic training there. Together with Joseph Buttinger — who was the president of the central committee of the Revolutionary Socialists in 1935 — she supported the political underground movement with the help of money and fake passports. Her apartment was the illegal center of the Revolutionary Socialists (...) After fleeing back to the US, Gardiner and Buttinger became more involved in psychoanalytic pedagogics as well as politics«

(Kaufhold 2003 b). She »played a decisive role in keeping psychoanalytic pedagogics alive in the American exile« (ibid.).

As another example, Esther und William Menaker should be mentioned. Both of them studied in Vienna from 1930 to 1935 and completed their psychoanalytic training there (cf. Menaker 1997). »Among other things Esther Menaker worked at the *Burlingham-Rosenfeld School* and she taught a few analysts English in order to make the emigration easier for them« (Kaufhold 2003 b).

Besides the varied international contacts, some of which came along with the International Psychoanalytic Association (IPA), »the high academic and scientific qualifications and reputation contributed to establishing effective help quickly and opening up possibilities for flight and emigration« (Mühlleitner, Reichmayr 2003, p. 77). For instance, Ernest Jones stayed in direct contact with »the representatives of the British emigration office and he corresponded regularly with Anna Freud about questions of emigration and placement of the analysts from Vienna« (ibid.). Anna Freud spoke up »loudly for her colleagues«, but she »also voiced her doubts« (ibid.), probably because she knew her father's rigid attitude concerning this question. He played down the dangerousness of the Nazis and wanted to hold out in Vienna under all circumstances.

Sigmund Freud's illusionary assessment of the destructive character of the Nazi power is astonishing in so far as he intensively tackled the aggressive-destructive sides of the human psyche. The image of mankind created by the Freudian psychoanalytic theory is characterized by an especially pessimistic view. The human being seems to be a game ball of the dark side of human nature which is determined by sexual and aggressive-destructive drives (cf. Wirth 2001). Psychoanalysis calculates for the worst. Freud

(1930, p. 112) wrote in *Civilization and its Discontents:* »Men have gained control over the forces of nature to such an extent that with their help they would have no difficulty in exterminating one another to the last man. They know this, and hence comes a large part of their current unrest, their unhappiness and their mood of anxiety«.

Freud's theoretical pessimism was supplemented by a personal attitude one could call stoical and fatalistic. In a letter of 7 February, 1930 to Oskar Pfister, he defended his »pessimism« and emphasised that »the death instinct« was to him »no affair of the heart, but it seemed only to be an unavoidable assumption because of biological and psychological reasons« (Freud, Pfister 1963, p. 144). His fanatical and stoically-defiant attitude nearly became fatal. Some of the first Jews to leave the country — which was no longer theirs — were psychoanalysts like Max Eitingon, Otto Fenichel, Erich Fromm, Ernst Simmel, and more than fifty others (cf. Gay 1987, p. 665). Two of Freud's sons, Oliver and Ernst, who had already settled down in Germany, thought it was a good idea to emigrate. His other son, Martin Freud, stayed in Vienna together with his father and took part in the official funeral of Dollfuß in 1934, wearing the uniform of a lieutenant of the Austrian artillery. Martin Freud looked up to Dollfuß and also to his successor Schuschnigg, who seemed to be a guarantee for Austria's fight against Nazi Germany (cf. Freud, M. 1999, p. 210 ff). On 10 May, 1933 the Nazis set Freud's works on fire during a spectacular burning of books. Nevertheless, Freud held out in Vienna »in submission« (Freud, Zweig 1968, p. 76). »The only thing I can say«, he wrote in the summer of 1933 to his nephew Samuel, »is that we have decided to hold out until the end. Perhaps it will not be too bad« (quote by Gay 1987, p. 667). The Palestinian government (cf. ibid., p. 699), Ludwig Bin-

swanger from Switzerland (cf. ibid.), the English government, and even the despised American government offered Freud asylum, but Freud remained unaffected. The
Viennese psychoanalyst Richard Sterba und Freud's den-
tist, Josef Weinmann, visited Anna Freud in the autumn of
1937 in order to tell her their concerns: »We hoped that
our ideas would cause Anna and the Professor to leave
Austria before it was too late. (...) She stood firmly and
told us that the professor did not want to hear anything of
the sort and that he would not like to be bothered with
these ideas. He had decided to stay in Vienna and to die
where he had spent nearly 80 years of his life« (Sterba
1985, p. 162 f). Only after massive pressure from Ernest
Jones, Marie Bonaparte and others could he make up his
mind to emigrate. The main reason for him to give in was
that his daughter Anna had been interrogated by the
»Gestapo« and he feared for her life. With the help of the
American embassy in Paris, W. C. Bullit and the influential
connections to Marie Bonaparte, he literally managed to
escape in the last minute. Freud and his family fled to
Paris and then to England, where they spent the rest of
their lives. Four of Freud's sisters stayed in Vienna. Freud's
sister Adolfine starved in Theresienstadt and the three other sisters were probably murdered in Auschwitz in 1942.
Freud was not able to find out anything about their fate
(cf. ibid., p. 731).

In contrast to most of the other analysts, Freud did not
emigrate to the United States. His reservations about this
country were too great. In a letter to Zweig, he called
America the »Anti-Paradise« (Freud, Zweig 1968, p. 186)
and in a letter to Ernest Jones, »a gigantic error« (quoted
by Gay 1987, p. 633). »Between May and July of 1938, the
majority of the Viennese psychoanalysts left Austria«
(Mühlleitner 1992, p. 395). Elke Mühlleitner (1992) de-

scribed, in her book *Biographisches Lexikon der Psycho-analyse*, the biographies of the members of the Viennese Psychoanalytic Association: 23 emigrated to England, 3 to Israel, 62 to America, and 12 to other countries. 11 members were not able to emigrate. They died in ghettos and concentration camps (cf. Mühlleitner 1992; Mühlleitner & Reichmayr 2003, p. 80 f; Kaufhold 2001, p. 268).

Coping strategies concerning emigration

In the following section, we will give a detailed account about a series of interviews we had with Jewish emigrants who emigrated to America in their childhood and adolescence and who later became psychotherapists or psychoanalysts. The interviews took place during our 6-month stay in New York City in the summer of 2002. Three of our interviewees lived in Washington and Boston. Aside from San Francisco, Los Angeles, Chicago, and the Menninger Clinic in Topeka, these three major cities were the main centers where the emigrated analysts had settled down. All of the psychoanalysts we interviewed were more than 70 years old and most of them were still working. We held narrative biographical interviews in which emigration played a central role. The subject of our conversation was their life story and everything our interviewees knew about the development of psychoanalysis in America after 1945. We wanted to know how the emigrants dealt with the fact of emigration and the difficulties connected to it. We were interested in how forced emigration, persecution and expulsion had influenced not only their personal and professional lives but also their psychoanalytic and political attitudes and beliefs. At this time we would like to discuss these conversations. Some of our meetings had characteristics of research interviews. We recorded some of them on video; in others we took notes either during or after the interview. In some cases we met only once, but in others we met several times and some even developed into a personal relationship. We have based the following report on these interviews. We cite them extensively but we also express our own ideas and thoughts which we have developed in connection to these interviews.

Acquisition of leading positions

The group of emigrants, who were already well known analysts in Austria and Germany, were welcomed in America and highly respected. They remained in personal contact with their founding father, Freud, and were therefore highly esteemed. In the early years of psychoanalysis, not only many psychiatrists but also teachers and social workers from America traveled to Vienna in order to receive psychoanalytic training from those analysts who were later forced to emigrate to the US. Besides that, many of the psychoanalytic emigrants were very creative people who were inspired by a pioneering spirit and the enthusiasm of discovery in the 1920's and 1930's. They published numerous books and articles. In America, many of them acquired leading positions as lay analysts, control analysts, directors of psychoanalytic institutes, and dominating speakers in theoretical discussions. Anni Bergmann, who was born in Vienna and lives in New York City, told us in an interview that »the emigrants had a dominating and partly limiting influence on psychoanalysis in America. They made many things possible but also hindered further development through their dogmatism.«

The American historian Paul Roazen also said during our interview that the European analysts who emigrated to America in the thirties had an enormous influence on the American psychoanalytic movement and psychoanalytic institutes: »Often the Europeans took over the leading positions and the American colleagues were stripped of their power.« What were the reasons for this development? Roazen: »First of all, the European analysts were directly connected to Freud and therefore possessed extraordinary authority. Secondly, many of the American psychoanalysts had traveled to Europe before the war in order to obtain their psychoanalytic training. When their former teachers, supervisors and training analysts fled to America, they automatically regained their leading position. The only barrier for the Europeans was the fact that their medical training was only partially recognized and only physicians were allowed to practice psychoanalysis as a clinical profession. The so-called »lay analysis« was not accepted. Therefore, the lay analysts concentrated on the training analysis of candidates, on teaching at the university, on research and publications, on the organizational development of the institutes, and on the treatment of private patients.«

We would like to point out that many psychoanalytic couples took over leading positions in some famous institutes: Helene and Felix Deutsch, Edward and Grete Bibring dominated in Boston, Jenny Pollack-Waelder and Robert Waelder in Philadelphia, Anni Angel-Katan and Maurits Katan in Cleveland, Edith and Richard Sterba in Detroit, and Marianne and Ernst Kris in New York City.

But the emigrants also took over leading positions on a theoretical level. The three most brilliant figures of American psychoanalysis all came as emigrants from Europe after World War II, from Vienna to be more precise: Heinz Hartmann, who was a member of the Psychoanalytic Association of Vienna, dominated psychoanalytic discussions with his »Ego Psychology« for more than three decades. His immense influence continued until the seventies. His influence decreased because of Heinz Kohut's theory of narcissism which became the most important psychoanalytic theory during the seventies and eighties. Kohut's greatest opponent, Otto Kernberg, emigrated to America as a child together with his parents. He discovered the borderline personality disorder and created a theory about it. On the one hand, he is characterized by the ability to bring people together who belong to very different psychoanalytic groups. On the other hand, he is also able to find a synthesis of very different theoretical concepts. It was not until the twentieth century that an American psychoanalyst, Stephen Mitchell, took over a leading position in theory. His theory »Relationality« emphasizes the existential dependency of human beings on social relationships (cf. Mitchell 2003).

It is important to mention Erik Homburger Erikson, who was born in Frankfurt, grew up in Karlsruhe and got his psychoanalytic training in Vienna, and also Erich Fromm, who was born in Frankfurt as well. Their similarity was to open psychoanalysis for the social science. This brought them enormous resonance in cultural studies and social sciences, but made them outsiders within the psychoanalytic associations and in Fromm's case resulted in expulsion from the International Psychoanalytic Association.

The emigrants used two almost conflicting strategies in order to work through the trauma of leaving their homeland. One strategy was to openly get through it by having a strong will and by assimilating as quickly and smoothly as possible in their new environment. In contrast to many other emigrants, the psychoanalysts were welcomed by their American colleagues with either open arms or with great admiration. This enabled many emigrants to make a rapid career in the land of unlimited possibilities. A New York psychoanalyst Martin Bergmann, who was born in Prague, told us: »Most of the analysts who emigrated were very successful. It was better for them in America — much better than it could have ever been for them in Austria or Germany.« However, for the rapid adjustment to the American way of life, they had to pay a price: Many emigrants developed a defense of mourning so they would not feel the suffered loss of their homeland, relatives and possessions. Many of them denied the fundamental psychological shock caused by the Holocaust. For the last 20 years many different studies have been published (cf. Jacoby 1985; Reichmayr 1990; Mühlleitner 1992; Fallend & Reichmayr 2002; Reichmayr & Mühlleitner 1998; Fallend & Nitzschke 2002; Kaufhold 1993, 1994, 1999, 2001, 2003a; Bergmann 2000a) »concerning the traumatic effects of the expulsion of the sciences psychoanalysis and psychoanalytic pedagogics into American exile« (Kaufhold 2003a, p. 38). There is no doubt that the »extraordinary creative beginning phase of this reform movement« (ibid.) during the 1920's and 1930's, which seems to be socially engaged, democratic as well as revolutionary, was damaged and destroyed because of the trauma of expulsion.

Roland Kaufhold has emphasized that »the discussions about the impact of the expulsion of psychoanalytic pedagogics and psychoanalysis did not pay enough attention to the fact that through the emigration, many analyses were suddenly ended, which resulted in additional traumas«. Richard Sterba described the extreme situation vividly: »It was important that we left Austria as quickly as possible as long as the borders were still open (...) I had to risk being stopped at the border. Of course, we had to inform all of our analysands and psychoanalytic candidates that we were leaving Vienna. As many of them had come to Vienna to receive training at our psychoanalytic institute, they understood why I would leave a country where psychoanalysis could no longer be taught. The others could not be spared the trauma of the sudden termination of their analysis« (Sterba 1985, p. 165f). »This also applied to Bruno Bettelheim, who — after many years of therapy — had started his training analysis with Richard Sterba« (Fisher 2003; Jacobsen 2003).

However, not all of the European psychoanalysts were met with a pleasant reception in the praised land on the other side of the Atlantic Ocean. Like other emigrants, the psychoanalysts were victims of culture shock and misunderstandings (Jacoby 1985, p. 149), and in some of the psychoanalytic institutes they were confronted with competition and distrust (ibid., p. 157). Otto Fenichel, who observed the tension between the Europeans and Americans, noticed the strong competition among them and reported the hostility towards strangers (Mühlleitner & Reichmayr 2003, p. 84).

The second strategy to help deal with the trauma of emigration was to cling to the familiar ways of living and thinking of their former world and to vehemently defend these beliefs against all doubts which were brought up through their new cultural experiences. The idealization of their homeland and of their lost cultural connections represents a general defense strategy of the emigrants. The psychoanalysts were also not immune to it. For instance, Jacoby wrote that Otto Fenichel did not shy away from »confessing to the soul and the literal of European psychoanalysis. He watched every analyst who assimilated zealously, very skeptically, and criticized their »blatant denial and self-denial« (ibid.).

Both defence strategies are characterized by the attempt to deny the painful experience of losing their homeland through dogmatisation and ritualisation.

In spite of their obvious contrasts, both defense strategies encouraged a development which Russell Jacoby (1985) called »the Americanization of psychoanalysis« (ibid. p. 166) and »the triumph of conformism«.

Above all, he meant the medicinalization and psychiatrization of American psychoanalysis and the loss of the culturally critical tradition of psychoanalysis.

If one looks back, Freud's hostile opinion of America was confirmed. He had »almost obsessively« advocated the opinion that »the American civilization was threatening his invention because it had subordinated itself to a psychiatry which acted in a pragmatic manner« (ibid., p. 150). Paradoxically, the dogmatization and theoretical petrifaction of psychoanalysis were essentially formed by the emigrants from Europe. In the year 1937, Heinz Hartmann had already established the theoretical basis of this development.

Theoretical rigidity as a defense against the experience of expulsion and of the Holocaust: The Hartmann Era

Heinz Hartmann gave a lecture on Ego Psychology and the difficulties in adapting (*Ich-Psychologie und Anpassungsproblem*) at the Viennese Psychoanalytic Institute in 1937, the night before Hitler's march into Austria (cf. Richter 1995, p. 50). In 1939 his programmatical work was first published in the International Journal of Psychoanalysis and Imago (»Internationale Zeitschrift für Psychoanalyse und Imago«). In his memoirs, the Viennese psychoanalyst Richard Sterba (1985, p. 162) described Heinz Hartmann's lecture as »the last meaningful event during the meetings«

of the Viennese Psychoanalytic Association. This event took place at a time when the Viennese psychoanalysts had »increasing fear and worry« (ibid.) and »anxiety about our future« (ibid., p. 161). In his lecture, Hartmann founded the psychoanalytic Ego Psychology, which dominated the theoretical discussions and the identity of the International Psychoanalytic Association (IPA) for several decades. From 1940 and into 1970 there was hardly any psychoanalytic publication which did not quote Hartmann and his co-authors Ernst Kris und Rudolph M. Löwenstein. Martin Bergmann (2000a) even wrote about a »Hartmann Era«. As Arlow (2000, p. 86) emphasized, Hartmann's influence on the theoretical discussions was nearly undisputed, but in the clinical discussions the local dominating leading figures could maintain their influence.

Heinz Hartmann, who was born in Vienna, considered psychoanalysis explicitly as a natural science. He created several new psychoanalytic concepts: of the »conflict-free (autonomous) Ego Sphere«, the »autonomous ego functions«, »adaptation«, and »adaptational functioning«. While he emphasized the necessity of »adaptation« and the »adaptational functioning«, he developed a counterpart to the horror of the Holocaust, which just had come into the consciousness of humanity. Nobody wanted to be confronted with this issue — neither the victims nor the culprits, not even those who were not directly involved but were only witnesses (cf. Moses & Eickhoff 1992). In many aspects, Hartmann's denial theory was a symptom of a collective defense which characterized not only the psychoanalytic community but all intellectuals and society as a whole (cf. Bergmann 2000a; Richter 1995). By concentrating on the »conflict-free« ego development, one could establish a defense towards the Nazi theme by denying the concrete political circumstances.

Like every system which relies on denial, Hartmann's theory got tangled up in contradictions (cf. Fürstenau 1964; Horn 1979) and misjudged reality. Only by dogmatization could one maintain this theory. Subsequently, there was a trend in America during the »Hartmann Era« to be more and more conservative and orthodox in psychoanalysis which was mainly supported by the immigrants. The theoretical rigidity of many immigrant analysts can be described, according to Martin Bergmann (2000a), as a defense against the confrontation with the National socialist persecution, especially the Holocaust. Harold Blum (2000, p. 90) points out the paradox that on the one hand, Hartmann attached importance to adapting to reality, but on the other hand, his whole theory is distinguished by the denial of central aspects of political reality of his time: »National socialism, the war and the Holocaust were given no attention« (ibid., p. 90). According to Blum, the Holocaust is one of the two events which characterize the last century. The other one is Hiroshima and the threat of a »nuclear Holocaust« (Blum 2000, p. 91).

Two of the most influential researchers in the field of psychoanalytic Holocaust research are the couple Maria and Martin Bergmann. They run a psychoanalytic practice together in New York. Our interview with Maria and Martin Bergmann took place in their practice located on Fifth Avenue on the 14th floor — with a fantastic view of Central Park.

Martin Bergmann emigrated from Czechoslovakia to Palestine as a child in the 1920's together with his parents. According to him, he is not a refugee in a strong sense. His parents had to leave all their possessions and their house behind in Prague, and he lost several distant relatives in the Holocaust, but he does not feel like he is a Holocaust survivor. Nevertheless, he has been intensely engaged in

Holocaust research for decades. He has published books and articles relating to this topic and works with patients who survived the Holocaust. He has spoken not only to victims but also to the children of Nazi culprits. The child of a high-ranking Nazi has even become a good friend of his. He describes how dealing with the subject of the Holocaust has cost him a lot of energy. »I have recovered by writing a book about the History of Love« (cf. Bergmann 1987).

Maria Bergmann, who was born in Vienna, came into contact with psychoanalysis as a child. Her mother worked in a home for difficult children as a psychoanalytically trained therapeutic teacher. This is where she met Anna Freud.

> »When I was thirteen years old, I helped my mom in the home. I have been familiar with psychoanalytic thinking since I was a child. My father was a Professor of Mathematics. I grew up in a solid middle-class environment. As a child, I attended the Children's Conservatory and played piano. My family was a well-adapted, intellectual and a Social Democratic family. The ideas of the youth movement played an important role in our lives. In 1938, when the Nazis invaded Vienna, suddenly everything was different. We realized that we did not belong there any more as Jews. Suddenly we felt like a foreign body. My father was forced into a Jewish high school. I was about 15 years old. At that time, my uncle was the chief of police in Vienna, even though he was Jewish. Therefore, we felt safe. We thought the Nazis would not do anything to us because he could protect us. Soon we realized that this was not the case. I put pressure on my parents to emigrate, but the older generation found it difficult to leave behind the things they were used to. It was easier for my generation to leave. I even took off and left Vienna and went to Switzerland illegally. For a few months I hid there with the help of some Social Democrats but the danger was considerable. If I had been discovered, I would have been deported to Austria and the Nazis would have shot me immediately. In the end, my whole family was able to emigrate to England and then to America.«

In the 1970's, Maria and Martin Bergmann founded the »Group for the Psychoanalytic Study of the Effect of the Holocaust on the Second Generation«. For many years, together with other psychoanalysts, they dealt with the question what psychological effects the Holocaust had had on the survivors and their children and later published the book *Generation of the Holocaust* (Bergmann, Jucovy & Kestenberg 1982).

When we asked her what it had meant for her to work so intensely on this topic, Maria Bergmann answered: »It was not as satisfying as you probably imagine. During that time I had many sleepless nights. I could only read books like Hanna Arendt's *Eichmann in Jerusalem*. If I read in the evening, I would cry and could not fall asleep. But the intensive confrontation with this topic was very important to us. We also analyzed many patients who were children of survivors. That was very valuable and enriching for us personally. We also learned many fundamentals about the meaning of traumatization.«

To our question about how psychoanalysis had dealt with the experience of the Holocaust, Maria Bergmann answered spontaneously: »Not at all! Psychoanalysis denied the Holocaust totally. One analyzed the dreams like one did before the war, as if there was not a war, the flight, the fear and the Holocaust. Many years later, Western European psychoanalysts opened our eyes about what meaning the Holocaust had for our patients and for psychoanalysts themselves.«

Question: »Did you really first get the idea to focus on the Holocaust from Europe?«
Maria Bergmann: »After the war, the first generation of the psychoanalysts could not deal with the Holocaust at all. The analysts were not even interested when their patients wanted to share their stories about it.«
Question: »So naturally the patients openly denied this process ...«
Maria Bergmann: »... You are right, most of the patients did not want to talk about the Holocaust. But even if some of them wanted to discuss their horrible experiences — which also occurred — the analysts were then only interested in their childhood and their relationships.«
Question: »Could you tell us who was the first analyst who talked about the Holocaust?

Martin Bergmann: »The first analyst from Germany who talked about this topic was Ilse Grubrich-Simitis. She came to America as a candidate and introduced a case study about the treatment of a Holocaust survivor. All of the analysts were amazed: ›She is German but not a Nazi‹. I am even affected by it today. And even today it brings tears to my eyes.«

Martin Bergmann seemed to be affected emotionally, but he got himself together again immediately. Ilse Grubrich-Simitis' revelation must have occurred at the end of the 1950's or at the beginning of the 1960's. She was, at that time, the only one who would talk about the Holocaust. But after a while, a few Americans, in particular Judith Kestenberg, traveled to Germany. The great change, however, first took place at the international congress of the IPA in Hamburg in 1985. »It was very important for all of us.« It was the first congress of the IPA to take place on German soil, 40 years after the end of the National Socialists' reign. Some other Jewish psychoanalysts told us how important this congress had been for their opinion of Germany. The opening speech by the mayor of Hamburg, Klaus von Dohnanyi, especially impressed many of them deeply (cf. Dohnanyi 1986) and convinced them that Germany had really left National Socialism behind.

In fact, several psychoanalysts even wrote about the Holocaust shortly after the war. For example, Bruno Bettelheim had already given an account of his experiences in Concentration Camps in 1943 and he improved his publications during the 1950's and 1960's. His two books were called »The Informed Heart« (1960; German: »Aufstand gegen die Masse«, 1964) and »Surviving and other Essays« (1979; German: »Erziehung zum Überleben«, 1980). Since he was not officially recognized as a psychoanalyst in the United States but only as a psychoanalytic educator at the Chicago Institute, he was probably never considered a »real« psychoanalyst. His insecure status at the edge of the established psychoanalytic business served as a rationalization so no attention would have to be paid to his work.

In 1999 Martin Bergmann initiated a conference concerning the »Hartmann Era« (Bergmann 2000a), in which the main task was to analyse the overwhelming influence of Hartmann's theory. The contributors came to the conclusion that Hartmann's theory led to a theoretical and clinical dead end. The enormous influence of this theory can only be understood as a defense mechanism which helped the psychoanalytic community avoid dealing with the Hitler reign and the Holocaust.

The fact is surprising that in the early sixties, a critical and very differentiated discussion about Hartmann's theory had already taken place in Germany (cf. Fürstenau 1964; Horn 1970, 1971; Richter 1995). Neither Bergmann nor any other American author took notice of this discussion. Since 1964, Peter Fürstenau has argued that »the thoughts of Hartmann were to be seen as a scientific answer to a certain historical situation« (ibid., 154). »Hartmann separated the ego from the conflict between the drives and society« while he reduced »society to a biological and statistical environment« (ibid., p. 153). »Anything that was scandalous Hartman pushed into the background in order to put the similarities into the center« (ibid.). Therefore, Hartmann's concept of psychoanalysis fell behind Freud's and he adapted it to a non- or pre-analytical psychology which focused only on the conscious and denied the unconscious.

As Fürstenau points out, Hartmann's biological thinking leads, »on the one hand[,] to an idealization of the ego in the sense of a conflict-free and affect-free pure conditioning, and on the other hand to the idealization [and reduction] of society in the sense of a constant (normal) social developmental incentive« (ibid., p. 152). Even though Hartmann did not deny the meaning of the economic, political and social factors, his abstract and formal way of dealing with these problems produced the opposite effect. The concrete contemporary political and social situation in Europe led to a social ›enviroment‹ in which the most-willing-to-adapt analyst — Jewish or not — still could not adapt« (ibid., p. 155). This consequence was completely denied. Fürstenau gets to the point: »For many people adaptation led to death and destruction« (ibid.).

As much as the theoretical necessity of adaptation was emphasized, the majority of the psychoanalytic community after the war was characterized by dogmatism, rigidity, and an atmosphere of the fear of deviation. At the same time, psychoanalysis celebrated astonishing success at the psychiatric hospitals and at the universities. Hartmann's intention »to help free psychoanalysis from its scientific isolation by a widespread discussion with other sciences and to help make it easier for psychoanalysis to be admitted into the academic institutions« (ibid., p. 154) was very successful. Hartmann chose a very successful strategy of pushing everything problematic into the background by stressing the common ground and ties. In contrast to that, the Hartmann Era affected the internal discussions in a paralyzing and intimidating way.

After World War II, the fear of deviation was widespread among the psychoanalytic community. The former co-worker and co-author of Margret Mahler, Anni Bergmann (who was not related to Maria and Martin Bergmann), named prominent examples: Donald Winnicott und Margret Mahler. Winnicott was treated »terribly« by the establishment of the New York Psychoanalytic Institute when he gave a presentation there. The sentiments against him were »openly hostile« even though he had been invited by the institute. »I am absolutely sure that Winnicott would not have been accepted as a member of the New York Psychoanalytic Institute at that time if he had had such a desire. Luckily, that would not even be imaginable today. In the meantime, the atmosphere has become more open and more tolerant. The biggest change started when the court decided to allow psychologists to become psychoanalysts as well.«

In hindsight, it is very astonishing that Margret Mahler, the internationally recognized and, even at that time, very famous psychoanalyst in the field of child analysis (cf. Mahler 1985), always feared being thrown out of the American Psychoanalytic Community. Anni Bergmann suspects that because of this fear of isolation, Margret Mahler »was, in a certain way, very rigid«, also when she tried to develop her own thoughts. Actually, the fear of being thrown out was widespread during the psychoanalytic movement.

Perhaps the rigidity of the psychoanalytic movement has to do with an »identification with the aggressor«. Psychoanalysts practiced the mechanism of isolation under which they had suffered themselves as Jews. Another aspect resulted from the history of the psychoanalytic movement and its inner dynamics, which was characterized by isolation from the very beginning. These processes of externalization and splitting can be understood as a result of the archaic topics which the psychoanalysts had to deal with since the early years of psychoanalysis, but which were not fully understood in this time period, especially in their archaic and preoedipal dynamics. The fears, which were triggered by the unconscious dynamics, caused regressions and splitting of the group (cf. Wirth 2000). Perhaps the creation of psychoanalysis is connected to the (not completely successful) attempt to cope with the problems associated with being an outcast, which characterized the situation the Jewish people were in (cf. Freud 1925, p. 110).

Individualism as a coping strategy

Another strategy to deal with the demands of emigration was to make oneself independent while avoiding a close attachment to only one group. We were often faced with this strategy in our interviews. Frank Lachmann, who immigrated to New York, also used this strategy, which could be described as individualism: »The polarity between affiliation and expulsion played an important role my whole life. I always tried consciously and unconsciously to belong to various groups instead of belonging to only one group. I always avoided attaching myself to only one group in order to keep all of my options open. To build bridges was more important to me than to emphasize a certain position. For example, I was interested in infant research as well as in psychoanalysis and tried to find out how one side could profit from the other.«

Individualism is not only a chosen way of life but can also be a psychosocial attitude which is caused by an emigrant's fate. The fate of always being an outsider and never being able to get rid of these basic feelings has stamped the life of psychoanalytically oriented psychotherapist Gisa Indenbaum. We talked to her in her practice in New York City and spoke in English. In fact, German is Gisa's native language but since her parents are not alive anymore, she hardly has the opportunity to speak German and therefore has forgotten many words. She has never gone back to Germany and has no desire to do so.

»My parents both came from Poland and emigrated to Germany after World War I. I spent the first nine years of my life in Berlin on a street called Grosse Frankfurter Strasse. I think it is located in the former East Berlin. My father was a hat maker. Over the course of a few years he built up a small factory in which he employed some workers. Financially, we were doing very well. My family belonged — as I would say today — to the upper middle class. I had — and still have today — a brother who is four and a half years younger than I am. My mother ran the household with the help of some employees and also worked in the hat factory. We were a happy family and lived in a larger community with friends of my parents like an extended family. I had a happy childhood and liked going to school because I liked to learn. But even at that time I felt like I was an outsider. Most of the time, I was the only Jewish girl in the class. I felt very isolated in school. For example, every morning when all of the children got up to pray, I was told to remain sitting. It wasn't like I had to remain sitting during the prayer, but I was allowed to make the decision. That was an important difference to me. At that age, I had to decide whether I wanted to make my differences visible by not praying or try to fit in by standing up and denying my Jewish identity. I was seven or eight years old at that time. I cannot remember what I decided to do, but I do remember quite clearly the inner struggle and the burning shame. These basic feelings of isolation and those of an outsider have been with me my whole life. Nevertheless, in Germany we felt secure through our extended family, which made me feel happy and safe. Except in school, I never had anything to do with non-Jewish children. My grandparents were still orthodox Jews. But for my parents, religion was not very important even though they still had a strong Jewish identity.«

Gisa stressed that her family was not assimilated. »My parents were Jews who lived a life of cultural Judaism.« Already from that time, she remembered moments which clarified the social position of the Jews: »I remember that even in 1933 there were organized riots against Jews. Jewish stores were destroyed and Jews were beaten up on the streets. I remember that I saw brown shirts marching down the street singing the ›Horst Wessel song‹ and I was scared. I think that was even before Hitler came into power.«

Hans-Jürgen Wirth: »You still do not belong to any of the established psychoanalytic institutes. Have you also remained an outsider in this respect?«

Gisa Indenbaum: »Yes, in a certain sense. But you have to take into consideration that I was already 50 years old when I finally finished my Ph. D. in psychology. I had gone to school all my life and therefore I did not feel like going through well-organized psychotherapeutic training again. Instead, I looked for a few supervisors and psychoanalytic teachers who had different theories and views. I went to their seminars for several years. I learned from traditional psychoanalysts, Bion followers, object-relationship psychologists at the Melanie-Klein-Institute, and was also engaged in family therapy.«

Trin Haland-Wirth: »How did you become a psychotherapist?«

Gisa Indenbaum: »That took a long time. During the day I worked in a factory to earn money and in the evening I went to school to finish my studies. I got married, had three children and got divorced in 1962. Luckily, at that time college was free. At New York University (NYU) we mainly focused on Freud and I liked that. I did not ever personally meet the big names like Erich Fromm, Theodore Reik and others but their spirit was still present ...

Should I tell you how I first came in contact with Freud's works?«

»Of course, we would be very interested in that.«

Gisa Indenbaum: »When we fled from Germany and made a stop in Lisbon, I often went to the library to read. I had an older friend who was already studying. He told me about Freud, so in the library I read Freud. He wrote about all these issues which were like my own. He described the feelings, fantasies and problems I was familiar with and was not able to talk to anybody else about. At the age of sixteen, I fell in love with psychoanalysis.«

Hans-Jürgen Wirth: »Did psychoanalysis help you understand yourself better?«

Gisa Indenbaum: »Yes, my isolation made me feel sad and lonely. I often thought about myself, and therefore was fascinated with psychoanalysis. Interestingly enough, reading made me feel less lonely because I found out that I was not the only one who had these feelings, thoughts and fantasies. There were also other people who thought and felt like I did and had to struggle with the same fears and problems. On the one hand, I was a very sad child, but on the other hand, we were also happy and celebrated many parties and picnics. This was the only way to survive. The Jewish community in Lisbon was very helpful. There were many refugees, who were planning where they could emigrate. There was even the idea of buying a boat to flee to North Africa, but again, we were very lucky. We had the chance to emigrate to the United States. The financial and professional beginning in America was very difficult for all of us. We all worked in a factory. My father, who was used to being self-employed, had a hard time working in a position where he had to take orders. Actually, he was never able to get back on his feet. He tried various things, but they didn't really ever work. In the end, the reparation payment from the German government helped them get their retirement.«

The effects of September 11, 2001 on the psychoanalytic identity

In the summer of 2002, when we interviewed some emigrants in New York City, Boston and Washington, the terrorist attacks of 9/11 were always present. In nearly every conversation it was mentioned. This was also the case in our interview with Gisa Indenbaum.

>Have you completely assimilated?«
Gisa Indenbaum: »No, I have never completely assimilated. How could anyone assimilate anywhere with this history? The feeling of isolation and that of being an outsider can never be forgotten. Since New York is a city full of outsiders, it is the place where I feel the best. Nevertheless, I lead a life full of activities, friends and colleagues. Whenever I talk about isolation, being an outsider or my anxiety, that doesn't mean that I am terribly sad and lonely. I think there are some scars still remaining and that they will always be there.«
>Which influence did fleeing, persecution and emigration have on your life?«
Gisa Indenbaum: »These experiences have affected my life like a chronic disease. My attitude towards the world has also been influenced. And even my children have been affected indirectly. Take my son, for example, who does not live in New York City. He is a doctor and owns a large farm where he grows vegetables, raises animals, and works hard. After 9/11, he suddenly had a panic attack and felt threatened as a Jew. What exactly was he afraid of? I think his anxiety has to do with my experiences and those of my family.«
>How did you feel after 9/11?«
Gisa Indenbaum: »I was shocked. I was paralyzed for three days.«
>Did all the old memories from the time of persecution and fleeing come back?«
Gisa Indenbaum: »Yes, of course.«

It was interesting that nearly all of the emigrated psychoanalysts were critical about Bush's Iraq policy. In Germany, some people who supported the war argued that one has to learn from the failed appeasement policy of the Allied forces during Hitler's reign and therefore must fight against a brutal dictator like Saddam Hussein who is known to be a mass murderer. These arguments hardly convinced any of the emigrants we interviewed. Instead, most of them agreed with the German politicians Gerhard Schröder and Joschka Fischer, who did not agree with Bush about going to war against Iraq. It was actually embarrassing for them to tell us that they had a president who was not only a »Wannabe Cowboy« but also said: »We want bin Laden — dead or alive«. Nearly all of them criticized the severity of Sharon's policies against the Palestinians.

In these interviews with the psychoanalysts who had to emigrate during their childhood and youth from Europe to America, we recognized how strongly psychoanalysis on both sides of the Atlantic Ocean had been damaged and affected by the breakdown of civilization because of National Socialism and the Holocaust. The topics »Psychoanalysis and National Socialism«, »Psychoanalysis and emigration«, and »Expulsion of Psychoanalysis from Europe« have been dealt with in Germany since the end of the seventies, accompanied by controversial publications in the psychoanalytic journal »Psyche« and disagreements in the German Psychoanalytic Association (Deutsche Psychoanalytische Vereinigung, DPV). In America, there have also been several publications about »Psychoanalysis during National Socialism« since the seventies. The crucial question about the role of the emigrants in post-war psychoanalysis and the basic meaning of the Holocaust for the psychoanalytic identity, however, has only been identified in the last few years (cf. Bergmann 2000a). It is of central importance for psychoanalysis, as a historical and reflexive science, to deal with these questions. Psycho-analysis is preoccupied with the biographies of the subjects in their historical context and therefore psychoanalysis has to realize its own growth as a historical process.

Translated by Kerianne Shewring and Hans-Jürgen Wirth

THE IDEA OF MAN IN PSYCHOANALYSIS: CREATOR OF HIS OWN LIFE OR SUBJECT TO THE DARK INSTINCTUAL SIDE OF HUMAN NATURE?[1]

The traumatic birth of the human being as an anthropological prerequisite for creativity and failure

Creativity, which is one pole of our subject, comes from the French *creature* and the Latin *creatura* and means to create. The creature is the creation. Instinctively, one thinks about the story of creation: according to this story, the human being is only partly a creation of God — he created the other part himself when he ate from the tree of knowledge. When Adam and Eve were still living in the garden of Eden in complete harmony with nature, they found themselves — writes Erich Fromm (1963, p. 367) — »in nature like an embryo in a womb. They were humans but at the same time they weren't«. As soon as they ate the fruits from the tree of knowledge and disregarded God's orders, they cut through the umbilical cord that had tied them to Mother Nature. Human beings partly

[1] One part of this article was previously published in: The Psychoanalytic Review. Special Issue on Death edited by Jerry S. Piven, Vol 90, Number 4, August 2003, p 583-596. Another Part was previously published in: Jerry S. Piven (Ed.): The Psychology of Death in Fantasy and History. P 137-162.Westport 2004 (Praeger)

unhinged themselves from their complete instinctive natural characteristics, and through that disposed of — at
least partially — the laws of nature and became the very
first human beings, i.e. living creatures, which distinguished themselves from other living creatures mainly by
the fact that they had control over their decision-making
and the freedom of will, and that they also knew about
their being »thrown into the world« (Heidigger), i. e. their
own finiteness. With the loss of paradise entered the
awareness of death into the life of the human beings. The
Myth of Creation allegorically describes the premature
birth of man, his crudity, his defectiveness and the traumatic circumstances of his incarnation. The early expulsion from the heavenly abode in the womb is a process of
»divisiveness« — to speak with Schelling — due to which
the oneness with Mother Nature is disrupted. The »tear-
ing-away« (Schelling, quoted by Böhme & Böhme 1996,
p. 147) from nature, from »absolute liquid« — says
Schilling —, and the »bodily fear« experienced during this
time (Böhme & Böhme 1996, p. 155) form the roots of
the human self-confidence.

The key word »divisiveness« points towards the other
pole of our subject, failure. In German, the word for »failure« (*Scheitern*) is etymologically derived from the word
Holzscheit (meaning piece of firewood) and literally means
»sth. which has been split«. One used to say about vehi-
cles or ships which fell to pieces that they had become
»Scheiter« (splits) (cf. Kluge 1989, p. 628). The existence
of man is distinguished by its split state: Man is a part of
nature and still he has transcended it; he stands in the
middle of life and still has an awareness of his own death.
Helmuth Plessner (1928) speaks of the »eccentric position« and the »world-openness« of man. Max Scheeler
(1926, p. 115) stresses the »immense fantasy excesses of

man over the environmentally-bound«. Since man is a »lacking-being« (Gehlen 1963) and »doesn't fit in any special environment instinctively« (Safranski 1994, p. 185), he must stick to his life goals and search his own ways of life. He has to compensate whatever is missing in him naturally at the societal level, which is created as culture, and at the individual level through considerate care and creativity. He has to »overcome his lack of specific adaptation through ›intelligence‹« (Scheeler 1926, p. 114).

The prize for his »eccentric position« is that he can fail at his self-determined goals. The reward for his »world-openness« lies in the possibility of being able to create his own life.

Creativity and failure are ways of existence that are only typical to man. They signify the tension between self-determined goals and what one can achieve in relation to these goals. Here, the ego ideal as the bearer of imagination, as we would like to be, is of central importance. Chasseguet-Smirgel, following Freud, has interpreted the ego ideal as the legacy of narcissism and as a substitute of the primary narcissistic absoluteness. Creativity provides a way of bridging the gap between the ego and the ego ideal. The creative work arises from the narcissistic need, the lost perfection, to reestablish the torn oneness with Mother Nature (Schelling) (cf. Chasseguet-Smirgel 1981, p. 98).

It is no coincidence that the creative act, which takes place in the character of the creator, is characterized metaphorically simultaneously as a procreation and birth act (cf. Auchter 1978). It begins with the first idea; the inspiration, which is often described as a lightening notion (Rauchfleisch 1990, p. 1127), turns into the resolution of this idea and into letting it grow in oneself until the birth of the creative work (ibid., p. 1122). In the self-descriptions of most artists, inspiration is character-ized as a »voice of the divine« or »voice of the uncon-scious«, as an inspiration that is implanted in the artist from an outside source while he is just the vessel (ibid., p. 1126).

This description also contains the natal metaphor. A pregnant woman is actually »just« a vessel for the child that she brings into the world, an event which is often described as a »miracle«. And in fact, during birth one may experience an emotion very similar to the deeply moving emotion one has at an extraordinary artistic event, for instance, a musical performance. Several au-thors see an important motive for doing creative work in men's envy of being able to give birth (Rauchfleisch 1990, p. 1122). According to Rank (1924–2000), howev-er, one could also regard creativity as an attempt to over-come the natal traumas. Kunz thinks »the creation of artistic works« is »to a certain extent a link between con-scious deliberate doing« that distinguishes man »and procreation and parturition« (Kunz 1975, p. 44 f), there-fore, unambiguous natural processes. In the philosophy of the Romantic period, particularly in Schelling, art is understood as an attempt of reconciliation with the ini-tial separation from nature.

Otto Rank's Psychoanalytical Approach to Creativity

Amongst the psychoanalysts of the earliest times, Otto Rank is the one who dealt with the topic of creativity most intensively. His book *The Artist* (1907), which the 23-year-old Rank published following Freud's recommendation, earned him a position in the circle of the first psychoanalysts around Sigmund Freud as the person responsible for the application of psychoanalysis to humanities. He consolidated this position through the first psychoanalytical doctoral thesis, *The Interpretation of The Lohengrin Saga* (1911), the extensive founding work *The Incest Theme in Literature and Saga* (1912), the books *The Double* (1914), *Psychoanalytical Contributions to Research of Myth* (1919), *The Don Juan Figure* (1922), and his book with Hanns Sachs, *The Significance of Psychoanalysis for the Mental Sciences* (1913). In his principal work *Art and Artist* (2000) he developed a wide-ranging psychologically philosophical framework on a psychoanalytical basis about the relationship of creativity and art, early experience and weltanschauung, individual and society. Rank investigated the human »creative drive«, the anthropological aspiration to express oneself in creative works — from cave painting to children's drawings, culminating in artistic work and the »creation of the human cultural works« (Rank) —, and to overcome fear of death with its help.

Rank's early discovery prepared the way for his later research, which found that there were many parallels between the birth motives of the mythological heroes and the birth dreams of many patients, which he investigated further in his book *Myth of the Birth of the Hero* (1909). In his book *Birth trauma and Its Significance for Psychoanalysis* (1924), he found the first formulations for the historic meaning of the earliest pre-linguistic, prenatal and during-birth experiences for the self-image of individuals and of human society.

In the end, however, Rank's new ideas were not accepted by Freud and his circle and led to his exclusion from the psychoanalytical movement and the complete tabooing of his entire works (cf. Janus 1998; Janus & Wirth 2000).

Psychoanalysis between the Enlightenment and Romantic Period

It became clear that in the dispute about the psychological significance of birth and the earliest mother-child relationship for the mental development of humans, two diametrically opposed ideas of man were clashing. Freud regarded himself as a scientist and his concepts were influenced by mechanistic ideas oriented towards the model of physics and physiology. In his philosophical convictions, he was committed to the ideals of Enlightenment. According to Freud's philosophy, not only the neurosis of human beings but also their entire inner life, culture and in the end even history are governed by an ensemble of biological drives. In Freud, the instinctual nature appears as the master of human conditions, as a creator of history. Following Schopenhauer, Freud understands the will of man as a blind will, the unconscious instinctual powers of id.

Besides the great cultural movement of the Enlightenment, Freud's thinking was furthermore shaped by another significant spiritual trend, whose influence Freud had denied in himself and fought against in his colleagues: the Romantic period. On the one hand, Freud's implicit philosophy follows the tradition of the modern natural sciences, its rationalism, its determinism, its belief in objective truths and in the liberty of value of science; on the other hand — as, for example, Henry Ellenberger (1985), Odo Marquard (1987), Michael Düe (1988), Werner Bohleber (1989), Carlo Strenger (1989), Hartmut and Gernot Böhme (1996), Günter Gödde (1999), and Martin Bergmann (2000b) have shown — it follows the tradition of the Romantic period and the romantic philosophy of nature. One can understand the Romantic period as a cultural countermovement to the Enlightenment, but one can also interpret it as its supplement and advancement. While the Enlightenment proclaimed the values of reason and society, the Romantic period cultivated a culture in which feelings, dreams, the unconscious, the irrational, and subjectivity of the individual occupied a central place. The Romantic period opposed the view that everything human was measured only against the scale of reason (cf. Gödde 1999, p. 35) and it revalued feelings, senses and passions. It emphasized inspiration, spontaneity, intuition and an extremely heightened ability of feeling and called for an understanding of other cultures, other historical epochs, and even of nature. As Ellenberger (1985, p. 289) demonstrates in his study about *The Discovery of the Unconscious*, there »is hardly any concept in Freud and Jung that was not anticipated from the philosophy of nature and from the medicine of Romanticism.« If the motto of the Enlightenment was: »Have the courage to use your reason«, then the motto of the Romantic period could be: »Have the courage to use your feelings«. According to the contemporary view of psychoanalysis, both of these mottos should be indispensable to the psychoanalytic position. Freud denied the romantic tradition of his thinking, and this led to his falling out with those of his colleagues whose ideas were especially strongly shaped by romantic thinking — particularly, Carl Gustav Jung, Sandor Ferenczi, and Otto Rank.

However, a secret tradition of romantic thinking exists in psychoanalysis which ranges from Ferenczi and Rank, via Michael Balint and W. D. Winnicott, to Heinz Kohut and self psychology. It is true that this tradition has already been laid out by Freud himself; however, its denial and fight deprived psychoanalysis of its most creative minds because it caused the repeated division of the psy-

choanalytic movement (cf. Wittenberger 1995). Furthermore, these disagreements were traumatizing and as a result, they caused bans on one's thinking, taboos, inhibi-
tions of scientific creativity that have an effect even today
(cf. Wirth 2000). Otto Kernberg (1998) has recently described »Thirty Methods for the Suppression of Creativity
in Candidates of Psychoanalysis« in a satire.

There are numerous indications to show that Freud's
personality was that of a Romantic: the passionate love
letters to his bride (around 1500 in 4 years) speak just as
romantic a language as his effusive relationship with Wilhelm Fliess. The romantic philosophy arises from his
identification with the character of the lonely hero Robin-
son, who on the one hand »settles down as comfortably as
possible« in »splendid isolation« (Freud 1914, p. 22), and
on the other hand has to fight against an entire army of
enemies, just as it arises from the foundation of a »secret
committee« of six elected devoted students, who solemnly
committed themselves to defending psychoanalysis and to
whom Freud presented a ring as a symbol of their elec-
tion. Even Freud's identification with Goethe, his ideal of
beauty, his interest for art and archaeology and his literary
style is a piece of evidence for Freud's romantic attitude
towards life. Goethe's romantic and emotional hymn *Nature* impressed Freud so much »that I enrolled in medicine« (quoted by Gay 1989, p. 34). Finally, even his central theoretical concepts, the idea of the unconscious, the
meaning of dreams, his interest in »Primal Phenomena«
are absolutely inconceivable without Romanticism.

Erich Fromm (1977, p. 236) sees the most important
reason for Freud's extensive influence on culture in the
»fruitful synthesis« between »rationality and Romanticism«. The »creative power of this synthesis« (ibid.) becomes clear when one compares the theories of Freud with

those of Adler and Jung, who — each in his way — would have resolved this synthesis again in favor of the original differences: Adler returned to a »one-sided rationalistically optimistic theory« (ibid.), while Jung lost himself in romantic mysticism. Freud, however, is enlightened and romantic at the same time — even though he denied his romantic side himself. Freud's Romanticism is »shattered Romanticism« (Marquard 1987). His romantic sides are hidden behind his skepticism, his rationalism and his almost demonstratively accentuated pessimism. »The nature that was stressed and empowered by Freud is not ›romantic nature‹ anymore, but ›instinctual nature‹« (ibid., p. 226).

Freud and the Poets

Even Freud's attitude towards poets and artists is shaped by his ambivalence to Romanticism and characterized partly by his envious devaluation and partly by a romantic and effusive longing. This becomes exemplarily clear in his ambivalent demeanor towards his Viennese contemporary Arthur Schnitzler, who was also a doctor working from home and who, at the same time as Freud founded psychoanalysis, became a writer of worldwide fame. Freud contacted Schnitzler after hesitating for a long time. When Freud congratulated him on his 60th birthday in his letter dated 14th May 1922, he made the following confession to him:

> »I have tormented myself with the question why I never really made an attempt in all these years (...) to have a dialogue with you. (...) I believe I avoided you out of a kind of doppelgänger shyness. (...) When I immersed myself in your beautiful creations, (I have consistently) believed to have found behind their poetic appearance the same assumptions, interests and results that were known to me as my

own. Your determinism as your skepticism (...), your being moved by
the truths of the unconscious, of the instinctual nature of man (...), all
this affects me with uncanny familiarity.«
»So, I have gained the impression that through intuition — actually as
a result of fine self-perception — you know all the things which I have
had to discover in other human beings through an arduous process.«
(Freud 1960, p. 339)

Freud's »doppelgänger shyness« is connected to the »uncanny familiarity« which he feels towards Schnitzler. If we
consult Freud's explanation of the uncanny (Freud 1919),
the feeling of the uncanny makes itself felt because »the
well-known, the long-familiar« (ibid., p. 231), »the secret-
ly-well-known that has experienced suppression and re-
curred from it« (ibid., p. 259) strikes one as being odd.

Doppelgänger has an uncanny effect — Freud (ibid.) —
because it personifies »all the omitted possibilities of
shaping fate which fantasy still wants to hold on to, and
all the tendencies of ego which could not prevail as a result of outside adversity« (ibid., p. 248).

Apparently, Freud sees the realization of wishes, fantasies and a literary-creative potential in Schnitzler's character which he would have liked to have developed himself.
On 1st April 1884, 28-year old Freud wrote to his bride:
»You will be astonished to hear that I feel poetic inclinations...« (quoted by Jones 1957, III, p. 485). Schnitzler
represents Freud's own suppressed identity as an artist
and writer that is foreign and familiar to him at the same
time and therefore seems uncanny to him (cf. Worbs
1983, p. 180). Against this background, Freud's ambivalent de-meanor towards Schnitzler becomes comprehensi-
ble. In spite of all of his admiration, he devaluates
Schnitzler in a subtle way by allowing him intuition and
describing his works as »poetic appearance«, whereas he
does not grow tired, in regard to his own work as a scientist, of stressing the arduousness with which he researches

reality without illusions. Freud sees himself as a worker of the spirit, as the »medicus who tortures himself with the understanding of neuroses every waking moment« (Freud, quoted by Worbs 1983, p. 191). Freud makes this even more clear in a letter to Martha dated July 11, 1882. He writes:

> »I think there is a general enmity between artists and us workers in the details of science. We know that in their art they possess a picklock which unlocks all feminine hearts effortlessly while we usually stand helplessly in front of the strange symbols of the lock and torment ourselves to find even one matching key«. (quoted by Jones 1957, I, p. 139)

In Freud's view, an artist is an easygoing fellow to whom the knowledge as well as the favors of the female hearts come easily and effortlessly — that is, through intuition — for which the earnest, down-to-earth and realistic scientist has to struggle every single day.

Freud's idealized admiration for the poets and artists also becomes apparent in the following words: The discoveries of psychoanalysis »about the meaningful nature of dreams«, writes Freud (1907, p. 33), had already been anticipated by »the poets«, whose »evidence is supposed to be highly regarded because they maintain that they know a lot of things between heaven and earth of which our bookish wisdom wouldn't let us dream.« »Even in psychology«, Freud says further, »they are far ahead of us ordinary people, because they create from sources that we still haven't developed in science. (...) they are also worthy countrymen« (Freud 1907, p. 33). Although Freud was ready to acknowledge artists as worthy countrymen, they never became his equal partners in the process of knowledge gain. In the end — that was his conviction —, science would even open up the sources of artistic productivity, and do so without forming any illusions. Freud could not explicitly formulate that illusions do not only stand for lies and self-deception but — as creative fantasies, as countertransference fantasies, as free associations — they can also contain a much deeper knowledge about reality than distant scientific contemplation, even though this attitude thoroughly shaped his clinical practice.

Perhaps therefore, he had to resignedly determine that to him the deeper »character of the artistic achievement (...) remained psychoanalytically inaccessible« (Freud 1910, p. 209). In his study about Leonardo da Vinci (Freud 1910), Freud specifically writes that he could not explain the artist's genius: »We must acknowledge a degree of freedom here that can no longer be resolved psychoanalytically« (ibid.), only to grant a place to the »organic basis of the character« and »biological research« again only a few sentences later (ibid.). And in another place, he writes succinctly: »It is not a question of psychology to determine where the ability to create comes from in an artist« (Freud 1913, p. 417). In spite of all his admiration for poets and artists, Freud stuck to his opinion that »the scientist would have the last and decisive word over the poet« (Stein & Stein 1987, p. 32). Incidentally, Freud confessed to similarly kept limitations of his empathy towards the »dark continent« of feminity, towards the »oceanic feeling« (Freud 1930, p. 422) and towards music (cf. Gay 1989, p. 193). This profoundly marked not only Freud's understanding of art but also his idea of man and of human creativity. At an intellectual level, this inability is connected to the denial of the influences of Romanticism and, at a biographical level, to his own traumatic birth and his conflicting relationship with his mother (cf. Wirth 2000).

As much as Freud admired art, it was still an »illusion« (Freud 1933, p. 173) to him, »a mild anesthetic« (Freud 1930, p. 439) similar to religion, however, »harmless and agreeable« (Freud 1933, p. 173) »because it finds its right to exist in its compensatory function in the face of the relentless challenges of life« (Worbs 1983, p. 201). With his undermining of art as a harmlessly naïve, ineffective and uncritical organization, Freud underestimates, however, that art can be hard work, often containing social criticism — true art always contains an element of cultural criticism — and that art can also bring about reality-altering consequences; therefore, by no means does it have to be only »harmless and agreeable«. Freud becomes almost set on an absolute belief in the universal validity of the laws of nature and in the strict predetermination of all events. He cannot admit a view which allows creativity and free will a place in life since he uses his scientific distance as defense against his denied wish of »poetic freedom«.

The investigation of the unconscious in the 19th and 20th century does have its most concise formulation in psychoanalysis; however, artists of the Romantic period — like Arnold Böcklin —, romantic writers and poets — like Schnitzler —, and even philosophers of the Romantic period — like Schelling, Carus, Hartmann and Nietsche — have prepared the ground which first made the psychoanalytical discovery of the unconscious possible. Thus, one of the remarkable features of many pictures of the romantic painter Arnold Böcklin is a romantic-melancholic mood which has parallels in some of Freud's compositions — e.g. in *Transience* (1915a), *Keeping in Time with War and Death* (1915b) and in *Sorrow and Melancholy* (1916) (cf. Erdheim & Blaser 1998, p. 194). This mood arose through Freud's approach towards the unconscious, and because of his exceptional literary abilities he was able to generate the same spiritual mood even in his readers. Not only do his medical histories read »like short novels« — as he once realized in astonishment — but his theoretical treatments also partly move the reader into a state of mind which one only knows otherwise from reading literary texts. Freud (1895, p. 225) writes:

> »(...) it still affects me strangely that the medical histories I have written are like short novels, and that they are, so to speak, devoid of the serious character of scientific nature.«

Freud's fear — not to be recognized as a scientist — could be a reason for his denial of the romantic influences. He wanted to commit himself completely to the Enlightenment, rationality, natural sciences and determinism.

Interestingly, Schnitzler was plagued by the same problem, namely, the apparent incompatibility between science and literature. Schnitzler's conclusion »My works are nothing but diagnoses!« is a formulation that compliments Freud's statement (cf. von Boetticher 1999). Both writers felt committed to the positivistic scientific ideal and confused by this new way of gaining knowledge for which they had developed neither a scientifically theoretical legitimization nor a new idea of man yet. Rank, on the other hand, aggressively developed the romantic tradition of thinking denied by Freud in which psychoanalysis works as well. This was reasonable to him because he wasn't a doctor or scientist but regarded himself as an arts scholar and — in a broad sense — as an artist. The arts background and the identity of an artist allowed him the Freudian concept of »healing by becoming aware« to expand the idea that man only attains »spiritual well-being« when he »is capable of devoting his complete creative power to life and to the shaping of life«, when he places »his creative powers directly in the service of character development« and consequently achieves »complete bliss of character creation«, as Rank writes in his book *Art and Artist*. Rank's criticism of Freud's ambivalent idea of man opens one's eyes to the fact that creativity belongs to the fundamental opportunities of man which, among others, enable him to find a way through neurosis and psychological illness. Rank understands neurosis itself — similar to Alfred Adler — as (failed) creative achievement.

Sublimation between Defense Mechanism and Creativity

Oddly enough, Freud's idea of man was conflicting: On the one hand, he viewed human beings as strictly predetermined by their drives, recidivism and the »Heavenly Powers« (Freud 1930, p. 112) — Eros and death instinct. On the other hand, the goal of psychoanalytical cure is the liberation of human beings from neurotic recidivism and unconscious entanglement by increasing their awareness.

In Freud's energetic model, all the energy comes from the id while the ego has no energy supply of its own. Ultimately, the ego does not have any place in Freud's model; it is not the ›master of its own house‹. However, he does not stand by the position that the human mind is to be regarded only as a derivative of drive strictly throughout — fortunately, I would like to add —, but leaves a few — if only small — loopholes for the mind, intentional consciousness, creative power, creativity. One of these loopholes is characterized by the term *sublimation*. Freud writes: The sexual drive puts »exceptionally large amounts of energy at the disposal of cultural activities and (...) as a result of its particularly developed characteristic — the ability to alter its goal without considerably increasing in intensity. One calls this ability to exchange the originally sexual goal for another, a non-sexual but psychologically related one, the ability to sublimate« (Freud 1908, p. 150).

The aspect of sublimation brings up an alternative component in Freud's Personality Model which Freud, consequently, did not formulate in detail. One partly gains an impression that Freud wants to conceptualize sublimation in such a way that the fate of drive becomes conceivable, which make the rights of an individual reconcilable with those of society. In sublimation, a person gains his rights because he does not have to suppress his sexual wishes while at the same time, the interests of society are taken into consideration. In this respect, sublimation makes a contribution to culture. But then again one runs into formulations according to which, man is entirely at the mercy of his blind instinctual nature and the ego remains helplessly caught in-between drive, superego and reality.

Freud's difficulties in looking at his own concept of the instinctual nature of man from a critical distance become understandable against the background of the great philosophical, cultural and political controversies. With his instinct theory in particular, Freud succeeded in making an epochal breakthrough in the self-conception of man. Most importantly, Freud broke away from the tradition that was strongly influenced by Christianity. Almost inevitably, Freud the innovator had to begin in an area that had for centuries been subject to the strongest suppression: sensuality, physical urges, naturalness of man, as it was — above all, the so-called »animalistic«, »sinful« in man which, according to Christian belief, was an obstacle in the way of attaining eternal salvation (cf. Kunz 1975, p. 250). As a result, Freud is, admittedly, in danger of making the physical urges absolute and debasing the other side of the human being — his »intellectuality«. Here, the intellectuality of man represents his reflective consciousness, his freedom to make conscious, deliberate decisions and to execute his actions, his ability to create himself and to shape his life creatively. Only the co-action of these two powers — the natural roots in physical urges and the reflective distance of the consciousness on the one hand, and decision-making by free will and artistic creativity on the other hand — account for human existence in its constant endangerment, frailty, and tragedy (cf. Kunz 1975, p. 251; Schafer 1972). Even if the term sublimation has only played a marginal role in psychoanalytic discussion, it is of central importance for the explicit or implicit idea of man in psychoanalysis. If one classifies it as a sub-category of defense mechanisms, as Anna Freud does in her book *Ego and Defense Mechanisms* (1936), one mistakes the anthropological meaning of creativity. Freud was wise enough to leave unspecified whether he thought sublimation was a special kind of psychological mechanism. Fürstenau (1967) pleaded for the term *sublimation* not to be subordinated to defense mechanisms, in order to have any theoretical term at all which allows to conceptualize, on the one hand, non-pathological contact with physical impulses beyond direct satisfaction and on the other hand, renunciation of the impulses. Whitebook (1996) described sublimation as a »border term« which makes conceivable a reconciliation between drive and reason, between sexuality and spirit, between the intra-psychological and the extra-psychological. Creativity is based on the relatively little defined human sexuality and searches for a way for its satisfactory integration into the inner life. It requires a creative search for possibilities of sublimation because man could not become master of his surplus sexual energy, neither through direct satisfaction nor through its suppression. Creativity is therefore at the disposal of a sublimated integration of sexuality into the psyche and into object relationships, and conversely, creativity feeds on this energy.

Premature Birth as Anthropological Radical

Freud particularly acknowledged the extreme helplessness of man as a result of his premature birth in his essay
Inhibition, Symptom and Fear (1926), which was dedicated
to the critical examination of Otto Rank's Birth Trauma
theory:

> »The biological (factor) is the long-drawn helplessness and depen-
> dence of a small human child. The intrauterine existence of man
> seems to be relatively short in comparison to most animals; he is sent
> into the world more immaturely than others. Therefore, the influence
> of the real outside world is strengthened, the distinction of the ego
> from id is prematurely stimulated and the dangers of the outside
> world are increased and the worth of the object that alone can protect
> against these dangers and take the place of the lost intrauterine life,
> enormously increased. This biological moment thus produces the first
> situations of danger and creates the need to be loved, which never
> leaves man again.« (Freud 1926, pp. 168 f)

Premature birth and the extreme helplessness resulting
from it in turn has the consequence that socialization and
individualization play such a great part in the making of
man that they make a considerable contribution to the anthropological being of man.

Interestingly, Freud also mentions the need to be loved
as an outcome of the early need for protection and help in
man. To add to it, there would also be the complimentary
need to love, which is firstly and above all necessary on
the mother's side. The need of love in its passive as well as
its active form becomes, however, an anthropological
characteristic of man per se since this way, the necessary
supply of loving care, communicative response and recognition can be definitely guaranteed. I find it remarkable
that Freud makes, at least implicitly, a distinction in this
citation between love and sexuality. Apparently, love results primarily from premature birth and the need for re-

sponse in man, whereas sexuality results from the drive. How can the relationship between love and sexual drive be characterized? Both enter into an obviously close liaison, without, however, merging into each other at any time. Sexuality can use love to strengthen itself quite well but it probably would not be dependent on it. Conversely, the connection of love to the sex drive is justified because love, like a tender, sensitive and susceptible being, has — so to speak — searched for a robust and powerfully effective partner within the psyche so that it could establish itself permanently.

Because of his premature birth, man remains dependent on protection-giving and uterus-like objects, which are first provided in the form of the mother-child symbiosis and later in the form of human culture and human community. This is the starting point of Peter Sloterdijk's *Sphere-Work* (1998, 1999), in which he puts forth a hypothesis, with reference to Otto Rank, that man spends his whole life in bubbles, spheres and shells which are supposed to serve as lifelong substitutes for the amniotic sac, out of which man is driven too early. Any achievements of civilization and culture always have a function at an unconscious level, namely, to compensate for this premature vulnerability. Houses, institutions, families, groups, cultural systems, each of which constitute a miniature world, are substitute forms for the womb. Rank had already thought about all this in connection with the trauma of birth but later it was even more explicitly formulated and also explicitly misunderstood (cf. Janus 1994), e. g. by Freud who discusses the question whether Caesarian children are less traumatized than children who are born naturally (Freud in his letter to Ferenczi dated 03/26/1924, quoted by Wittenberger 1995, p. 312). As a result, the very far-reaching metaphoric function of birth trauma, especially its anthropological meaning, was overlooked.

But numerous philosophers have chosen the premature birth of man — mostly indirectly — as a central theme of their philosophical reflection about man. When Martin Heidegger, for example, characterized the human existence as »being thrown into the world«, he found a formulation in which anthropogenesis was understood as precipitate delivery and therefore the traumatic aspects of birth were specifically emphasized. Hannah Arendt, on the other hand, developed a »philosophy of birth (...), a philosophy of the beginning« (Safranski 1994, p. 425) in which she made »the bare truth about birth« (Arendt 1958, p. 215), the »factor of natality, (...) birth« (ibid., p. 217) the center of her definition of being a human being. Hannah Arendt writes: »The new beginning which comes into the world with every birth can show itself off to advantage in the world only because the newcomer has the ability to make a new beginning, i. e. to act« (ibid., p. 18). Arendt — similar to Rank and Sloterdijk — sees the fulfillment of need in the artistic work, which is »to offer earthly accommodation to the mortal human being« (ibid., p. 201), which is capable of surviving for centuries and even for thousands of years without losing its sense. Precisely because it is devoid of purpose and usefulness, a piece of art, in which »the mortal human being can find an immortal home« (ibid., p. 202), symbolizes the »steadiness of the world« (ibid.).

The Consciousness of Death as an Anthropological Radical

Otto Rank considered the consciousness of death and the urge to overcome fear of death important motivating forces for the development of human creativity and culture.

»We can read in the works of all times, from Gilgamesh, psalms and Sophocles to Schopenhauer and the existentialists, that wisdom begins with mortal fear, above all, with the omnipotent fate ›that raises man when it crushes him‹ (Schiller)«, writes Max Stern (1974, p. 901). Even Freud repeatedly devoted himself to death and particularly determined the general tendency towards a suppression of death: »We have shown the unmistakable tendency to push death to the side, to eliminate it from life« (Freud 1915b, p. 341). It is all the more astonishing that the knowledge of one's own death plays a secondary role in psychoanalysis. Freud's own remarks on this theme have been very contradictory. He writes in *Keeping in Time with War and Death*:

> »One's own death is (...) unimaginable and whenever we make an attempt, we notice that we just remain onlookers by it. Therefore in the psychoanalytical school one could venture to remark: Basically, no one believes in one's own death or, which is the same thing: Unconsciously, each of us is convinced of our own immortality.« (Freud 1915b, p. 341)

A logical and philosophical problem which has always been on the philosophers' minds is that one's own death is difficult to imagine and the thought of one's own death leads to paradoxes, but from this, one cannot conclude that the unconscious does not know about death.

Rather, one can assume, in accordance with the philosophers Max Scheeler and Arthur Schopenhauer, that man has an intuitive knowledge of death, in spite of a deep-rooted tendency to deny it. Since these opposites coincide in the unconscious, it may definitely be assumed that ideas of immortality and fear of death coexist in the unconscious.

In *Inhibition, Symptom and Fear*, Freud writes: »In the unconscious, the meaning of our term — destruction of life — does not exist. Something similar to death has never been experienced« (1926, p. 160).

It is astonishing that in numerous of his famous case histories, Freud almost completely disregards the fact that in interrelation with the development of their symptoms, his patients were indeed confronted with death in a frightening and painful way. Irving Yalom (1989, p. 81), who examined Freud's case histories from the studies on hysteria under this aspect, comes to the following conclusion: »Death pervades the clinical stories of these patients so much that Freud could have only omitted it in his demonstrations of the cases' traumas due to excessive efforts of carelessness.«

Freud does not want to allow the knowledge of death even to the child: In *Interpretation of Dreams* (1900), he writes: »The child does not know anything about the horrors of decay, of freezing in the grave, of terror of the endless emptiness (...). The fear of death is unknown to him« (Freud 1900, p. 260). Freud assumed that there was no consciousness of death in eight-year-old children. 36 years later, Freud's daughter Anna, who had worked with children during the German air raids on London, knew better about the child's psyche than her father. She writes:

> »One can say with certainty that all children that were over two years old at the time of the air raids on London were aware that the houses collapsed when they were bombarded and that people in the collapsing houses were often killed or injured«. (quoted by Yalom 1989, p. 111)

Even if developmental psychological knowledge about the term *death* in children is relatively sketchy even today, we do know today that children »are greatly preoccupied with death. (...) Death is a puzzle to them and one of their biggest developmental tasks consists of dealing with the fear of helplessness and destruction« and with fear of death

(Yalom 1989, p. 98). Some developmental psychologists are even of the opinion that sexual issues are of rather secondary importance in comparison to the subject of death. The consciousness of the inevitability of death — someone else's but also one's own — and fear of death must be regarded as an anthropological radical in man which has considerable influence on our conscious and unconscious inner life. Even Freud seems to agree with this view when he asks, at the end of *Keeping in Time with War and Death* (1915 b), »Wouldn't it be better to allow death a place in reality and in our thoughts which it deserves, and to emphasize our conscious attitude towards death a little more which we have carefully suppressed until now?« And he ends with the recommendation: »If you want to brave life, prepare yourself for death« (Freud 1915 b, p. 345 f).

Elsewhere, Freud (1915 b, p. 343) speaks about our »relation to death (...) a strong effect on our life«. He holds a fiery summation for an absolutely fearless attitude which one could describe, following Michael Balint, as »Philobatism«:

> »Life becomes impoverished; it loses its attraction if the most important component in the game of life, life itself, is not allowed to be daring. It becomes as shallow and empty as an American flirt, from the outset of which it is clear that nothing will be allowed to happen, in contrast to a continental relationship, in which both the partners have to be constantly mindful of its serious consequences. Our sentimental bonds (...) make us averse to finding dangers. We don't dare to take the number of undertakings which are dangerous but actually essential into consideration, such as attempts to fly, expeditions into faraway countries, experiments with explosive substances. (...) The tendency to shut out death from life's calculations brings so many other sacrifices (...) in its wake. And yet, the motto of the Hanseatic League was: (...) one needs to sail but one does not need to live.« (Freud 1915 b, p. 343)

In this passage, Freud imagines the spiritual state of the philobaths in epic breadth and with obvious pleasure, as it was described by Balint and compared to the »ocnophile« clinging type. Actually, the philobatic and ocnophile attitudes represent two sides of the same coin. The basis is a dependence-separation problem which is typical of the anxiety-neurotic. Type A pacifies his fears of death and separation anxieties by clinging on to an object while Type B takes refuge in pseudo-autonomy under denial of fears of death and separation anxieties (cf. Richter, Beckmann 1986). Balint produces a connection between the philobatic type and the world of fun fairs and adventures which matches Freud's seafarer idea. As biographical studies about Freud have shown (cf. Jones 1957; Krüll 1979; Möhring 1985; Richter 1992, p. 77 f; Wirth 2000; Kollbrunner 2001), Freud suffered from different psychosomatic symptoms. His phobia of traveling, his separation anxieties, his fears of death, and his magical belief in the occurrence of his own death on certain dates — which he repeatedly had to postpone to the future because he survived the dates predicted by him — allow the conclusion that he was suffering from cardiac psychoneurosis. His massive fears of death made it difficult for Freud to acknowledge the problem of death appropriately, and caused his contradictory theoretical remarks about death.

Theoretically, fear of death leads Freud back to castration anxiety, but he then concedes that one should not overestimate castration anxiety because it »could not be the decisive factor for the female sex, which is certainly more disposed towards neurosis« (Freud 1926, p. 173). »Especially in the case of women« (ibid.), the most effective cause of fear of death remains the danger of loss of an object. Freud's conception is questionable for several reasons:

1. As we know from developmental psychology today, knowledge of death and fear of death arise earlier than the Oedipus complex and castration anxiety.

2. It is unlikely that fear of death has a different structure in females than in males (cf. Stern 1974, p. 924).
3. Castration anxiety is less existential than fear of death. One could say, better castrated than dead.
4. Children are actually confronted with death, whereas castration exists only in fantasy.

Therefore, the opposite may rather be the case: castration anxiety might lead back to fear of death. Max Stern (1972, p. 924) suspects that »in both the sexes, (the) castration anxiety has its origin in the trauma of the disappearance of self in case of loss of an object (...) Castration anxiety could be explained as the defensive postponement of fear of death, of being destroyed, to the genital.«

And following Rank (1924), one could assume that the trauma of birth is experienced as »something similar to death« (Freud 1926, p. 160). The life of human beings on this earth, therefore, begins with the elementary experience of death.

Let us look at these dynamics in the Oedipus myth. Oedipus' parents have decided long before his birth to kill their child if it is a boy. Oedipus is thus doomed even at the time of his conception. Immediately after his birth, he is confronted with death through the murderous intentions of his parents, who abandon him with his feet pierced. Oedipus suffers extreme birth trauma through the cruelty that is inflicted on him by his parents. Already at birth, he is confronted with human aggression and a readiness to kill that does not spare even one's own children. Even as a new-born, Oedipus is exposed to an extreme and realistic fear of death. He is an early-disturbed child; furthermore, he is an example of the significance of early deadly dangers and anxieties of death. After all, he is probably someone who was given an intuitive knowledge about the existence of death in the journey through life.

Basically, there is very little castration anxiety to be felt in Oedipus: Oedipus faces his father irascibly and uncontrollably and kills him and his companions without further ado. One could object, of course, that he is defending himself against castration anxieties by reversing them into activity. But is it not much more reasonable to assume that during the encounter with his father, Oedipus' death anxieties and their reversal were reactivated into murderous impulses? Because the father had not been able to utter castration threats against Oedipus yet; he had, however, attempted to kill his son.

The significance of an awareness of death is also visible in the fact that Oedipus is able to solve the riddle of the sphinx. In the riddle of the sphinx, one has to guess which creature walks first on four, then two, and finally on three feet. The acme lies in the fact that one can only solve the riddle if one has an awareness of the weakness of human beings, the finite nature of life, and the inevitability of death. Oedipus, who has been confronted with death since birth, knows about the existence and inevitability of death; he can look death and the deadly danger represented by the sphinx straight in the eye and is therefore able to solve the riddle. The Oedipus complex and the castration anxiety connected with it owe their central position within psychoanalytic theory to their association with early traumatization, the resulting fear of death, and awareness of death — factors of psychological development which Freud could not see in its complete range because of his own biographical limitations.

According to Otto Rank's concept, the development of specific human creativity contributes towards fear of death being alleviated so much that the knowledge of death can be integrated into life.

The superego is not simply an inheritance of the Oedipus complex but has a forerunner — as Melanie Klein suspects — in the pre-oedipal age as well. It is also an inheritance of the symbiotic relationship with one's mother and father, respectively, which is introjected as a power that is designed to protect against death (cf. Stern 1974, p. 925). One could also speculate about whether the superego is an anthropological constant in human life which could have developed from man knowing about his death, having a certain amount of freedom to make decisions in life, and from him being brought into this inevitable »tragic situation« (Schafer 1972) and guilt being evoked. It corresponds to the basic idea of »idealistic« philosophy ranging from Plato to the existentialists to award man the ability for creative self-realization but also for failure and self-destruction. The philosopher Pico has formulated it very pragmatically:

»The dog (will) always live like a dog and the lion will always live like a lion. Man, however, does not have a nature that compels him, does not have a being that conditions him. Man creates himself through deeds, man is his own father. Man knows this one and only condition: the shortage of conditions, freedom. His compulsion is the compulsion to be free, the compulsion to choose his own fate« (Pico, quoted by Kunz 1975, p. 104).

If one overexpands this idealistic philosophical thought, it certainly becomes wrong. Our topic here is precisely the fact that man is, and remains, part of nature and that he must often experience this close connection to nature very painfully through frailness of the body and mortality. On the other hand, the thought also seems to be irrefutable that man emancipates himself from nature and his own naturalness to a certain extent and attains an extent of freedom which is not available to the animal. It is interesting to see where Freud stands with regard to this question. In his

explicit philosophical comments he most strongly emphasizes the lack of freedom of man, his predetermination
through the fateful forces of impulses, and the extreme predetermination of his behavior. But on closer examination,
the latent anthropology of Freud's psychoanalysis is not too
clear: Freud's term *sublimation* could channel the libidinal
and even the aggressive drive needs into ways which would
be more beneficial not only for the individual but also for
its culture. The future role of reason, the faint but persistent
voice of the intellect could impart so much strength to the
weak ego that it could still become the ›master of its own
house‹. Working with grief could lead to the early, inevitable traumatizations being dealt with so extensively that
they would lose their compulsive character. The development of specific human creativity could contribute to fear
of death being soothed to such an extent that the knowledge of death could be integrated into life. And finally, psychoanalytic therapy and psychoanalytic enlightenment in
general could lead to the unconscious becoming conscious
and, through it, the unconscious active recidivism losing its
behavior-governing power. As we see it, the idea of man in
psychoanalysis is really not so one-dimensional but also
contains some starting points which emphasize the funda-
mentally available potential of freedom. But it is also certain that Freud evaluates the capability of man for freedom
as well as his responsibility for himself rather skeptically.

Creativity and Failure as Human Modes of Being

Creativity and failure constitute modes of existence that are
typical to man. They indicate the tension between a set goal
and what one has achieved with respect to that goal. There
must be a will that wants to reach something in the future

so that one can focus on something. The aspect of will and future has not yet been given much attention in psychoanalysis. Free will has been replaced by drive in psychoanalytic theory. And Freud was not concerned with the future as he was convinced of the all-determining meaning of the past. Death, however, is an inescapable factor that lies in the future and has a far-reaching influence on our present life. Denial of death invariably leads to an unfulfilled and superficial life which is determined by the »false self« according to Winnicott. The defense against listlessness, restlessness in the pursuit of gratification of sexual urges (Stern 1974, p. 926), the superficiality of life goals are an expression of a desperate attempt to keep the existential fear of death in check. Only those who are aware of the finite nature of their lives can go about being creative with their lives. Schopenhauer, Heidegger, Sartre and even Freud have always stressed that only a steady awareness of one's own death bestows the ability to man to do everything in life. One could modify Freud's citation »If you want to brave life, prepare yourself for death« with regard to our theme as follows: »If life is supposed to be shaped not by failure but by creativity and creative power, prepare yourself for death.«

Creativity, group formation and the development of culture acquire a special meaning on contact with the fear of death. I will try to formulate these thoughts anthropologically: In contrast to animals, not only is man connected to his ancestors in the past and to his descendants in the future by his genes, but apart from this, by cultural tradition man is also connected to the past, present and future of human culture in a much more comprehensive sense. Not only can the single creative individual — one thinks of the genius — bequeath his special talent to his biological descendants as animals do, but his individual creativity flows into human culture through communication and tradition and has the potential to influence all present and future generations. Culture transcends the lifespan of an individual and the identification of an individual with the group with the help of tradition, and culture gives an individual the feeling of immortality. Through it, we live not only in the present but also in the past of the Romans, Egyptians, Greeks, in Sigmund Freud's time and in a Utopian future (cf. Stern 1974, p. 926).

Interestingly, many artistic works, for example in architecture, need several generations to be completed. Notre Dame, for instance, was only completed after 300 years of construction time. But by this example one sees an important motive — the wish of the creator to make himself immortal through his work. Creativity should not be narrowed down to the field of art. Architecture, scientific work and even completely different social fields require creative work. In art, in a narrower sense, creativity is the center of intentions, while in creative processes, for example in business life, creativity is only a means to an end. Nevertheless, there are artists who are only mildly creative, while there are business people who accomplish very creative results.

Creativity is not a strict alternative to neurosis. Even artists can be neurotic. They are creative as well as neurotic, which has caused Müller-Braunschweig (1974) to speak of a relatively autonomous »creative system«. This is accurate in as much as creativity and neurosis are two variables that are independent of each other. Sometimes creativity may be helpful in overcoming neurosis, but that is not necessarily the case. Therapeutic treatment of an artist often stimulates his creativity, and the fears of many artists that a psychotherapeutic treatment could dry out their creativity are unfounded. In fact, based on my experiences in the psychoanalytic work with artists, a psychotherapeutic treatment usually stimulates their creativity. But it might be the case that creative productivity has a neurotic origin. In this case, successful psychotherapy will question the current form of creative productivity while, however, increasing the creativity of the artist altogether so that he can turn to other subjects or develop his creativity in other ways — even if others may not necessarily view this as creative progress. It may be more important for himself to focus his creativity on shaping his personality and his life than on producing artistic work in the traditional sense.

One of my patients, a talented painter and sculptor who underwent very good development during therapy that lasted for almost two decades on and off, explained that he was happy to have dispensed with creative works in the narrower sense. He experiences the creative process — becoming completely involved with himself — like a drug which claims him with every fiber of his personality, exhausts him and leads him to the limits of his possibilities.

The tragedy of human existence is a condition for the possibility to be creative as well as for it to fail. As Schafer (1972) argued, the task of psychoanalysis is to bring the analyzed and analyzer closer to the tragic dimension of life and make them aware of it. Life must be accepted as a tragedy in order to develop creativity on the one hand and to be able to fail on the other hand and to even accept this failure as a part of life. Failure is as much a part of life as creativity. Human beings who do not experience and accept life in its tragic dimension are denied creativity.

As Müller-Braunschweig (1984, S. 124) has emphasized, the creative process is characterized by »breaking open old structures and creating something new«. »This disintegration of old structures or problems and/or forms also corresponds to a temporary disintegration of inner mental structures« (ibid.), which leads to a process in which »regression and progression« take place »at the same time« (ibid.). »Therefore, the creative process leads to a new synthesis via a phase of weakening the personality and thereby is (...) related to the psychoanalytical process« (ibid.). According to Schafer, the psychoanalyst is a »self-made tool«. He writes:

> »A particularly important tragic element in the understanding of one's own role lies in the cognition of the analyst that he remains a self-made tool in spite of his bond with classical and well-sounded technical principles and therefore can only analyze in a way that is appropriate to him.« (Schafer 1972, p. 962)

A little later, Schafer speaks about a »creative element« in the analytical work, and he interprets »the life history« of a patient »which arises from analysis as a mutual creation of the patient and analyst« (ibid., p. 971). Psychoanalytic treatment itself is thus understood as a creative, inventive process, just as the training to become an analyst is a process of invention and creation of the analyst as an analyst.

One non-pathological possibility of handling unsatisfied needs, dreams, limits, losses, painful separations and the inevitability of death is creativity. The other, also non-pathological possibility is sorrow, which is a look at the inevitability of failure of ideas, hopes and wishes. By allowing sorrow over failure, we accept failure as an inevitable component of our life, and it is precisely this process which brings about the creative overcoming of failure. After sufficient grieving, there can be a life beyond failure. If grief is denied or suppressed, failure is fixated in trauma, which has to be repeated endlessly. Only the person who accepts his partial failure mourns it and thus integrates it into his life becomes free again, determines his own life, i. e. moulds it creatively. In this respect, creativity and sorrow are very closely linked. »Creativity is a form of handling the flaws of human life, a form of grieving which is triggered through life as death (...) But the creative individual is endowed with a specific ›ability to mourn‹ to soothe the pain about death, which begins at the moment of our birth« (Auchter 1973, p. 74). In a way, we have to mourn our own death for a lifetime, in the sense that we become aware of its inevitability time and again and that it becomes, so to speak, a part of our life. To accept the limitations of life, Freud had already realized, also means to attribute an increased value to our limited lifetime, to hold it in higher esteem as when one lives under the illusion that life is unending. Creativity freezes in rituals if it is not complemented by the process of mourning over suffered dreams or even over the limitations of one's own creative possibilities — even those of the current times, which even geniuses are subject to. Sorrow and creativity belong together. Creativity needs sorrow for further existence. Artists to whom due honor would not be granted until long after their death have always had to experience this. But this connection is valid generally. No creative work is perfect. There is no creation which has no critics, which will not be outperformed and put into a more relative perspective by the ravages of time. Only a creative person who dolorously accepts the imperfection of his work and his partial failure finds the strength to continue to be creative without his work leading to the ritual repetition of the same thing over and over again, i. e. getting stuck in recidivism. The term recidivism, which, in connection with death drive, takes on the character of a merciless »heavenly power« in Freud (1930, p. 506), could experience a similar extension of meaning as has already been bestowed upon terms such as transference, counter-transference and regression: All these terms partially have a positive creative meaning apart from the negative pathological meaning. Every repetition contains the possibility of new perspectives opening up through minute variations of the repeated fundamental conflict. Every repetition presents the attempt of revision and the further development of the original pattern of conflict. It is well-known that many artists work on the same conflict their whole life, which is a type of theme of their life. From this perspective, repetition is a creative act, which allows something unfinished to be seen again in a creative light. Not without reason is the principle of repetition a fundamental element of every artistic creation.

Just as creativity requires repetition and sorrow, the opposite is also true: Sorrow needs repetition and creativity. This is because only when the mourning process is experienced often enough and the mental powers reorganize and reorient themselves can the process of mourning really be completed, sorrow does not get consolidated into depression, and the psychic energies are once more able to devote themselves to the creative shaping of life.

Translated by Prajakta Sukhtanka,
with the assistance of Daniela Bone

About Family Dynamics and the AIDS Phobia. A Case Study[1]

The discovery and spread of AIDS have created a new neurosis: the AIDS phobia. Like almost no other disease in modern society, AIDS has become a metaphor (cf. Sontag 1989) that causes panic, fear and terror — and often also disgust, abhorrence and segregation impulses wherever people are confronted with it (cf. Richter 1987). Some people merely live in a state of exaggerated fear that they might be infected with HIV themselves or that their relatives could be infected and therefore practice strategies of phobic avoidance and precaution in order to handle their fears. Others, however, suffer from such high degrees of anxiety about getting infected with HIV that they reach delusional quality. The AIDS hypochondriac is unshakably convinced that he is suffering from a deadly weakness of his immune system and that this disease will soon be fatal. This fixed idea is accompanied by a constant state of anxiety. This drives the person to endless visits to doctor's offices and tests; a negative result of an HIV test provides relief only for a few days. The person avidly watches all the reactions of his body; the occurrence of common and usually harmless bodily symptoms such as fatigue, spots on the skin, swelling of the lym-

---

[1] A shorter version of this article was previously published in: Applied Psychoanalysis. Special Issue on Psychoanalytic Couple and Family Therapy, edited by David E. Scharff, M. D. & Jill Savege Scharff, M. D., 2003.

phatic glands, diarrhea, sweating at night time, slightly increased temperature etc. cause panic over and over again. Normally, this type of hypochondria is accompanied not only by psychosomatic problems such as insomnia, decreased work drive and life quality but also by severe relationship problems. On the one hand, AIDS hypochondriacs tend to be paranoid about being rejected and excluded by their family and friends and accept that as a just reaction to their imagined disease and punishment for their — usually single-occurrence — sexual »misadventure«. On the other hand, their behavior becomes increasingly incomprehensible for the people around them and therefore arouses criticism. Others cannot understand how the paranoid person can stick to his or her idea of suffering from AIDS in spite of having been tested negative a number of times. The fear of being infected with HIV is not only a psychological problem for the individual; very often it requires couple or family therapy.

To be precise, one has to distinguish between the *phobia of getting infected and the hypochondriac idea of already suffering from the disease*. As both forms tend to merge into each other, the inclusive term *AIDS phobia* has been used (cf. Jäger 1988). Finally, there is a third type of psychopathological reaction: the AIDS-paranoiac. It is justified to call a reaction paranoid when the fear of getting infected strongly involves »feelings of hatred for people who are infected that are experienced as some kind of persecutors and are sought to be fought« (Richter 1987). In a paranoid reaction, the psychosocial mechanism of »scapegoat projection« (Richter 1963) is essential. In order to control their own sexual conflicts by means of aggression, these people try to find groups of people on the outside who they can stylize as their enemies and fight. Naturally, we will see persons with this type of reaction less frequently in therapy. They prefer to project their fears onto politics and transform them into political convictions.

Those cases of AIDS phobia that fit the category of neurotic disease have reached a significant level in our society and must be considered a serious problem (cf. Ermann 1988). In AIDS counselling, Health Departments and AIDS support groups more often have to deal with phobic persons than with persons who actually are HIV-positive, suffering from manifest AIDS, or members of high-risk groups. A survey by the Public Health Departments showed that the »number of people who seek counseling because of exaggerated fear (...) exceeds 50% in every other Health Department; in every third, even 75%« (Floto, Fassl & Hettwer 1988, p. 643).

A representative survey on behalf of the BMJFFG (the German Department of Youth, Family Affairs, Women und Health), conducted by the Center for Psychosomatic Medicine at Giessen University, showed that worries in connection with HIV and AIDS are widespread in Germany. AIDS was found to be the cause of worry for more than two thirds of the 2,025 people interviewed. At the same time, there is a high degree of insecurity about the real extent of the spread of HIV. About two thirds of the population highly overestimate the spread of HIV. In addition, AIDS ranks among the most feared diseases, cancer being the only disease that is considered more threatening.

Because of the public attention paid to the new epidemic, and because of generously funded AIDS counselling, interest in the AIDS phobia has grown rapidly among psychotherapists and scientists. Theoretical studies (cf. Jäger 1988; Vollmoeller 1988; Hirsch 1989) have attempted to relate the AIDS phobia to other phobias, especially the well-explored heart neurosis or heart phobia (cf. Richter & Beckmann 1986), and draw information from the limited amount of literature about hypochondria (cf. Rosenfeld 1964, 1987, pp. 83 ff.; Uexküll 1974; Schilder 1926). All case studies that have been published so far (with the exception of Neraal 1988 and Woidera & Brosig 1990) offer only glimpses into the problem and lack the connection to family therapy. In view of the latter, the following extensive case study about the family treatment of an AIDS-phobic patient seems to be justified. It should offer insights into the dynamic of the AIDS-phobic individual, his family relations and treatment difficulties. Future studies will need to evaluate to what extent we can apply the data found in this case to the general characteristics of AIDS phobia. The political relevance of case studies like this lies in the possibility of adapting the psychodynamics of behavioral patterns in the microcosm of individual treatment to how the society at large deals with AIDS.

The Admission interview

Heiner's girlfriend scheduled an appointment for him by phone, telling the doctor that he was terrorizing his entire family with his fear of suffering from AIDS. The patient shows up alone for the admission interview. He is 32 years old and currently working as an engineer for the German National Railway Company. Although he is already balding, his boyish face makes him look younger than his age. He talks about his bodily symptoms, especially cold sweat, sweating at night, fatigue, skin lesions on his thigh, slightly increased temperature at night and burning sensations on his tongue. He is currently being treated at a hospital and has had several lesions on his thigh and two lymphatic glands removed. The operation has not changed his condition.

Spontaneously, he reveals that his mother's »over-pro-tectiveness« is significant for the family life. Both he and his brother used to be very much involved in sports, especially in the local soccer team. Since he fell ill, he has abruptly stopped all kinds of sports activities and started feeling »flabby«. He explains his mother's anxiety by the fact that her own mother died very early. As it is, his mother is not able to stay alone in the house at night even today. Her anxiety has had an inhibiting effect on everybody.

He describes his relationship with his father as good. The father also used to be a soccer player, and in earlier days they went to all the games together. By his nature, he is the exact opposite of Heiner's mother, namely, very tough and with a desire to succeed in sports.

Heiner has had a girlfriend for the last six years. They have a child together. It is quite unusual that he did not marry her even though they are from the same village. He has coerced her to move to the town of H. and that she live there together with him. This, however, did not go well. Their child, a girl, is now a year old. At first, his girl-friend's pregnancy was a shock to Heiner because he want-ed to be able to take advantage of being single a little longer. He describes the soccer team as a men's club noted for its chauvinism and enormous group pressure: »A man is everything. When the team goes places together, and af-ter the men have had some drinks after the game, each man wants to make the best impression on the women. As a result, people do things they don't really want to do. These men are really wild.«

I point out that he lives predominantly in a man's world, both in the soccer team and in his work as a rail-road man. The patient feels boxed into a corner and counters that he does not harbor homophobic feelings. I

tell him that I see a connection between the fact that the
AIDS virus is mostly carried through homosexual contacts, and my impression that he often feels repressed by
men but also attracted to them. He has the idea of spend-
ing a vacation together with his soccer team mates in
Ibiza, where, however, he has a one-night-stand with a
bar maid. This is the only opportunity for him to be infected by a person at risk. During the entire flight he experienced »hellish anxiety«. In order to mute his anxiety,
he got drunk before the flight. Altogether, he is an anxious type — not as extremely as his mother, but still very
cautious and health-minded. He does not smoke and
tries to lead a healthy life.

He has considerable feelings of guilt about sleeping
with the prostitute, saying that he usually dislikes such
things. He only allowed it to happen because he did not
want to be the odd-man-out and because he was drunk. In
general, he says that belonging to the soccer team has always driven him to fit in, so as not to appear as a »a weird
intellectual«. Therefore, he has always felt obliged to drink
and fornicate like the others in order to »be like one of the
guys«. He thinks that this fitting-in is actually dumb: »I
did things which I would have never done on my own. I
simply wanted to be one of them«. His whole family became involved with the soccer team. The guilty feeling
about Ibiza still nags him. Now he is very weak and he
feels that this is a punishment by God. As I comment on
the guilt feelings, he adds that guilt feelings constitute a
psychological problem. But this is overshadowed by the
HIV infection. He is convinced he is HIV-infected even
though all the doctors have told him that he is not. Therefore, he is full of anxiety and depression. He has a burning
sensation on his tongue and believes he has a fungus in
his mouth. He was operated on five times but with no suc-

cess. Partially, he also blames his parents: Had he married his girlfriend two years ago, he could have avoided Ibiza altogether. It is his fault that he allows people to influence him too much and that he does not listen to himself. Ibiza was actually »not his thing«. He is therefore profoundly ashamed of it.

Thoughts About Countertransference and the Therapeutic Situation

The patient is under considerable pressure caused by his suffering and seems to me to be motivated for therapy. He appears ready to talk and able to think critically about himself and his social relationships. He is able to arouse in me both sympathy for him and scientific interest in his »case«. He vehemently declines my recommendation to be admitted as a patient to a psychosomatic service because he has just started a new job and does not want it to be known that he is sick. Even though I think that inpatient therapy is indicated, I offer him outpatient psychotherapy in the hope of clarifying some of his family conflicts and to convince him to get interested in inpatient therapy in the future.

Overall, 16 sessions take place in five different therapeutic settings: after the first two interviews, the patient comes to the next two sessions with his girlfriend Karin. As it becomes clear how much he is still tied to his original family, I suggest to him that we be joined by his parents and his brother. After one family session without Karin, there are three more with her.

As therapy continues, the mother accepts my invitation to see me alone, and she comes for two sessions. During those sessions it becomes clear that for years she has been suffering from a massive anxiety neurosis which she has barely compensated by means of various family arrangements. By offering her individual therapy sessions, I intend to strengthen her insight into her illness and to take personal responsibility for her anxieties and her conflicts and not to burden her family, especially Heiner, with her psychosocial defense strategy. It is my hope that this will be a source of relief for Heiner.

In order to further Heiner's separation process from his parents, the five last sessions take place with the participation of Karin.

The Family is the Stronghold

The parents see the girlfriend Karin as the main cause of Heiner's problems. The father believes that Heiner's illness broke out after he got back with his girlfriend, who had left him three months earlier. The mother expresses a suspicion that Karin got pregnant against the wishes of her son, »in order to catch him«. Turning to her son, she says: »Be honest, you didn't want that child, did you?«. Heiner feels driven to agree with that. At the time, he was indeed overwhelmed by Karin's pregnancy. The mother believes that her negative attitude toward Karin is justified: »We only wanted the best for our son. Therefore, we had to be against her. Whenever she arranged something, she did so without our son's consent«. Besides, »it is a mean character trait« that Karin has so little consideration for her son and that she has left him before. He really deserves a better woman. She would not even prepare lunch sandwiches for him, despite the fact that he had to be at work all day long. And the fact that the son still brings his laundry to her house and often comes to her house for meals clearly shows that his partner is not really taking care of his needs.

The brother also speaks very negatively of Karin. For years, he has been against this relationship because he thought that »Karin is not attractive at all«. Today he claims to understand that »looks are not everything«. But he has heard negative things about Karin and holds it against her that has she left his brother in the lurch once. Therefore, he still holds on to his original opinion.

Commentary:

The father is probably right in his opinion that the AIDS anxiety broke out after Heiner made up with Karin. By embracing his girlfriend and the child, the patient has removed himself from his mother. This brought about deep unconscious guilt feelings in him. His AIDS anxiety is aroused by these guilt feelings and the punishment anxiety connected with them. It is a flight into illness from the conflict between his loyalty to his mother and his attachment to his girlfriend. His illness enables him to desert the battlefield. It also defends him from further reproaches by his mother because he appears punished and in need of mercy. At the same time, his death anxiety expresses a repressed rage against his mother. The »sick« body is both the punished self and the mother against whom his deathly aggression is directed. Without having his own personal opinion, the patient is caught between his mother and his girlfriend and feels as if he is in a »two-front war« which he can only lose. For six years, he has tried to »please everybody but gotten nowhere«. When he used to complain about his girlfriend, it was only to escape his parents' criticism. The patient feels »like a relay station« whose function it is to transmit from one side to the other what has been told to him. The illness now gives him the opportunity to see for himself what this is all about. By remaining ill and misunderstood, he is protesting his role as a relay station and thereby gains the strength to stand up for his opinions, even at the cost of self-injury.

Even though the position of the brother in the family is less precarious, he too seems to resort to rigid defensive strategies. I have the impression that the brother stubbornly sticks to his demeaning and wounding statements, in particular about »Karin's looks«, in order to prove that unlike Heiner, he is able to keep his distance, to be independent, to have his own opinions. He achieves this, however, at the cost of excessive harshness. Whereas the patient oscillates between different opinions, the brother compensates by being opinionated showing shades of brutality. Moreover, the brother overplays his anxieties, e. g. by keeping a BB gun under his bed when he is home alone.

The Mother-Son Relationship

The mother has the traditional role of the housewife in the family. She is submissive towards her husband, does her housework and is considerate of her husband and their children in every respect. She makes an effort to quickly quell any discord in the family. She falls apart when somebody is angry for a long time. She describes herself and her son in very similar terms. Like herself, Heiner is kind-hearted and quite different from his brother. She herself, however, is very prone to disappointment and when someone disappoints her, she remains offended and hurt for a long time. It happens to her often that her trust in people is not reciprocated. For example, once she was disappointed by a female co-worker to whom she had given support. Afterwards, she never associated with that co-worker again. She feels sorry for her son because he is so kind-hearted, unable to say no, and therefore gets exploited by his girlfriend. In response to my question whether she has been severely disappointed as a child, she talks about the sudden death of her mother, who died after the war from an infection in her tooth when she herself was 10 years old. From that time on, she has experienced anxiety which has not left her since. She is never able to be alone; she always needs someone around her. She is never home alone without »one of her three male defenders«. She says about the death of her mother: »I have no anger against my mother, but I was enormously disappointed«. Her own anxieties are so great, the mother realizes, that she really ought to be in therapy herself.

After her mother's death, her father never remarried. Therefore, it became very difficult for her to marry and leave her father. There have been big conflicts between her father and her husband caused by her father's jealousy of her husband. Shortly after they stopped fighting and her father was invited to live with them, he died. She claims that Karin would never be willing to take care of her in-laws in their old age. She, on the other hand, has submitted to her mother-in-law: When she got married, her mother-in-law told her that her son never used to polish his own shoes and that it should stay that way. The mother accepted this and now, in her own family, she polishes everybody's shoes as well. The mother expresses the fear that her sons view her as »the bad mother« when she doesn't pamper them.

Commentary

The mother's structural conflict is the same as the patient's. She, too, is ambivalently tied to her mother. Unconsciously, she still feels like the ten-year-old girl who, on the one hand, loves her mother and needs her protection, but on the other hand is deadly disappointed and hurt for having been abandoned by her mother. The unconscious hatred against her own mother reappears in the conflict with her co-worker and in the harshness and coldness which she shows towards her daughter-in-law.

Her statement that her sons might see her as the »bad mother« indicates that she harbors unconscious hostile images which contain death wishes, hatred, and resentment. Her »evil« self-image has come about through an interjection of her own »evil« mother, who disappeared suddenly. Since the age of ten, Heiner's mother has fought against her hatred of her mother by projecting all evil into the environment and by developing a special love, care, and sacrifice for her own family by means of a reaction formation.

The Father-Son Relationship

Father and son describe their relationship as harmonious and motivated by the same interests. In particular, soccer creates a special bond between them. They also read the same historical books. They do, however, occasionally have fierce discussions about politics, during the heat of which, the son has yelled at his father before that anyone who had such and such political opinions »deserves to be shot«. The patient rushes to explain that of course, he does not mean this literally. Then, he insecurely hints at differences of his with his father which he dresses in concerns about his health. He himself has tried to lead a healthy life, and he therefore often preaches to his father that he does not take good enough care of his health and he is far too heavy. The father has a »typical high-risk infarct personality«. The patient worries about his father and tries to get him to follow his advice.

When I point out the tensions between father and son, it turns out that the patient's decision to study engineering was actually his father's wish. Initially, the patient, following the example of an uncle, wanted to be a forest ranger. He took a difficult examination to be admitted to the forestry department and succeeded, but his father made him promise to give this career choice up. Actually, he feels sorry to this day that he did not become a ranger. In the present times, he feels wasted as an engineer whereas it makes more sense to him to be a forest ranger and fight for the preservation of the environment. The father describes himself as an ambitious man who, a displaced person, managed to enter high school but had to drop out just a year short of obtaining the diploma because of financial difficulties. In his job as an employee of the state, he feels both restricted and boxed into a corner. He was never able to achieve his goals. Therefore, he wants to warn his sons against »working for the state and committing themselves to a lifelong career as inspectors«.

The self-image of the patient is glaringly different from his father's. He describes himself as completely devoid of ambition. He no longer has ideas of a »big career« in his head, as he did when he still »harbored illusions«. He used to be politically active and considered entering politics: »Become the social secretary and do something — but I have given up on that idea«. Actually, he thinks this is sad and resigned, but perhaps it is the better way for him. It's the second best choice. He is now disillusioned, withdrawn into himself, and has developed an »employee mentality« of »personal security«. In fact, the patient works as an engineer for the State Rail System and has thus chosen a career as an employee »of the state« after all. His father has reacted to this decision with disappointment, but the mother has shown understanding for it.

According to the patient, his father has always attempted to bring him up to be a tough man. This became very important to him in playing soccer. He used to be a very hard player, ready to »play hardball«. He states that »earlier he used to be a soft player, then I consciously taught myself to be aggressive against the opposing team, to finish the opponent off«. Anyway, as an aggressive player, one is wounded much less frequently than when one plays softly and defensively. The patient agrees to my suggestion that perhaps in his opinion, this principle also applies to the rest of life. He is convinced that in life, the stronger guy is always the winner. Nevertheless, he has decided not to pursue the »career trip«. His father's education to manliness went so far that he threatened, »as a joke«, to shoot him if he ever were to find him holding a dust rag. As he tells this, the patient remembers how his father reacted contemptuously when the patient and his girlfriend were doing the dishes together one day and were surprised by an unannounced visit of his parents. When something like this happens, everybody in the family gets to know about it. The father particularly tells his own father about it, a man who also believes in men playing hard. Sadly, the patient reports that in his family he is considered to be a weakling and a softie.

Commentary

It is clear to me that the patient uses his acquired medical knowledge as a weapon against his father. At the same time, he flatters me by using a concept taken from the psychosomatic theory of illness, even though only hours earlier, he has expressed himself most critically about psychosomatic medicine. He is quite impervious to my psychosomatic interpretations of his illness, but he uses psychosomatic hypotheses as a weapon against his father. He hides his true feelings behind a complex system of strategies of denial, distancing, and turning statements into the opposite. I understand his worries about his father's health as a means of turning his aggressive affects into the opposite. Instead of feeling rage and hatred against the father — who, despite of the male predominance in the family, has left him at the mercy of his mother —, he worries that he might die from a heart attack. »Jokingly«, both of them admit indirectly that they would like to shoot each other.

It is obvious that there is a very close relationship between father and son. The father has powerfully influenced his son, e. g. by making him pledge his loyalty to him. The son subjugated himself to this in order to avoid aggressive conflicts with his father. When talking about that, the patient remembers that once his parents bribed him by paying for a vacation he was supposed to spend without Karin. He thinks the fact that he accepted that offer does not say much for his character strength. In order to please his father, he had to deny the softness, weakness and anxiety that his neurotic mother had inspired in him. He is trapped between his mother's anxiety-neurotic relationship and his father's ambitions. The patient embraces his parents' extreme differences, i. e. both »male« and »feminine« features. He is desperately trying to find a compromise between his father's and his mother's expectations.

An increased orientation towards his mother would result in arousing his symbiosis anxiety, whereas a more intense relationship with his father is not possible considering his passive homosexual wishes for subjugation. The patient feels contempt for his »feminine«, passive and anxious tendencies; he sees them as unmanly and weak, and ultimately as an indicator for homosexuality. His AIDS anxiety is connected to an unconscious homophobia.

Disguised as AIDS hypochondria, i. e. the idea of suffering from the »gay plague«, is the repressed softness, anxiety, and weakness. The patient has gained weight, lost his bulky muscles; he feels weak, is anxious — and thereby has turned into exactly the negative mirror-image of a man for which his father has made him feel contempt. By hurting himself, he is taking revenge on his father, who has been weighing him down with his extreme ideals of manliness and thus thrown back to his mother's mercy.

According to Richter's (1970) family typology, the patient's family is borderline between an »anxiety-neurotic« and a »paranoid family«. On the one hand, the heart-neurotic mother has organized the family as a protective world similar to a sanatorium (cf. Richter 1970, p. 75) ruled by harmony and togetherness. Conflicts and tensions are sought to be resolved as quickly as possible, and a healthy life style is supposed to ban all evil. Clinical studies actually prove that such a phobic family climate fosters heart neurosis and hypochondriac ideas in children (cf. Richter 1970, p. 72; Rosenfeld 1964, p. 219). On the other hand, the family has closed itself off from the outside world and projected all evil into Karin as a scapegoat. As the family is obsessed by the idea that all evil is coming from an outside enemy, the patient is able to sense aggressive conflicts only outside his psyche, and therefore projects all evil onto his body (cf. Hirsch 1989).

Thus, he tries to defend his girlfriend against his mother's accusations. His mother has always tried to find only negative things in Karin. She has always been the scapegoat for the family: »She was like a better Jew«. Often when he had done something wrong, the family would blame Karin for it.

The Treatment Process

In the course of the family sessions, the patient increasingly gains the ability to distance himself from his parents
and have his own opinions. However, his former excessively close relationship with his parents still impairs him.
When he would pour his heart out about his girlfriend
problems in he past during visits to his mother's house,
and tell her how comfortable he felt at his mother's house,
he provided her with the arguments she is now using
against Karin and to tie her son closer to her.

Over the course of the sessions, the father can finally
admit that »we are an exclusive group. We stand together
against outsiders«. It is possible to argue within the family,
but also necessary to make peace with each other. And,
yes, he admits, maybe they have seen »Karin as an intrud-
er«.

In the course of the therapy, the patient becomes increasingly able to stand up for his relationship and set up
boundaries between himself and his parents. About a year
after the beginning of treatment, Karin becomes pregnant
again and she and Heiner get married. Nevertheless, he is
still obsessed with his AIDS hypochondria and worries
that he might have infected his wife and his children.
While moderating his statements in the sessions when his
family is present, he tends to show off in the sessions with
his partner. His affects appear completely inadequate. He
alternates between laughing off his conviction of suffering
from AIDS and stating that he will die soon, or he talks
about his affair with an »alternative« woman. This woman
was much too challenging for him, especially sexually.
That is why he came back to his wife. He is a rather lazy
type that likes to be pampered. Apparently, the patient is
unaware of how humiliating all of this is for his wife. His

wife seems anxious and depressed and is often on the verge of crying. He does not respond to my attempts of confronting him with his aggressive and sadistic behavior. He sits there, straddle-legged, presenting his now big belly, laughs inappropriately, keeps constantly interrogating me and wants to debate medical matters with me. When his wife tells me how much she is suffering from the situation and that she herself has started to develop symptoms of anxiety, e. g. that she is not able to drive a car alone any more, the patient states that compared to him, his wife is mentally ill and needs psychosomatic treatment. In the future, she should come to the sessions alone, also to discuss the tensions with his mother without him being present. By this time, I have accumulated a great deal of anger inside me and can hardly stand the patient anymore. Now I blow my top. I confront him with his inappropriate laughter and his stupid talking. The patient instantly surrenders masochistically and states that he does not expect anything else but to be kicked out of their apartment by his wife and that it would be best to get a divorce. I confront the patient with the fact that his wife has demonstrated sufficiently that she does not want a separation but wants to communicate with him — but that, apparently, is not possible on that day; he has not uttered a single word in earnest, just dumb and superficial stuff. I give free expression to my emotions, although I do not believe that I engaged in counter-acting out. I believe that it is only possible to touch the patient inwardly by such a direct and strongly affective confrontation.

Soon after that, our conversation does actually take a positive turn. The patient stops his silly grinning and starts telling me something very personal. When he was a child, he was seriously ill twice. Both times, it was a near-death situation. One time, he was almost suffocated by a whooping-cough attack, the other time, he was seriously ill at the age of two. His mother feared greatly for his life. Upon entering puberty, he started to get closer to his father, to adopt his maxims of manliness. The patient talks about having fears of being alone in a forest as a child. Today, he is afraid of flying, taking elevators and all sorts of mechanical devices. Now I can talk to the patient about his feeling of being torn between his mother and his father, and that he actually does have a soft side which he just does not allow to develop due to his father's and his own adopted standards. He has tried to escape it by a macho attitude that actually does not suit him. The patient is able to agree with that, and for the first time, it is possible to talk to him about such things.

I chose affective confrontation as the therapeutic technique for this patient. Friendly and benevolent interpretations appealing to his ability to understand and his insightfulness have immediately been turned into defensive maneuvers by him. He keeps trying to get onto buddy-buddy basis with me. However, discussing matters rationally strengthens his defenses. That is also the case with other patients. Nevertheless, this is the first time that I have met a patient who keeps trying, stubbornly and cunningly, to set up such a disputatious atmosphere.

As I found out half a year after the termination of treatment, the patient's psychic state has become more stable. He is not as depressed anymore, can go to work and has started to exercise again. He and his wife have bought a house in a faraway town where he is working. In the near future, he plans to move there with his family. He has a distanced relationship with his parents and is now talking to them again after he had not been in touch with them for some months. Then, during a vacation he became sick with the flu and his temperature rose to 39° C. He was convinced that he was dying from AIDS and made his parents come and see him. Their relationship is now distanced but friendly.

Although the patient is now feeling much better, he has not given up his fixed idea that he is suffering from AIDS, and is still in touch with scientific institutes specializing in the treatment of this disease. There, they are busy testing him for some kind of virus that has not yet been identified and is probably unique to him. The patient speaks very well of the institutes; he feels accepted and taken seriously there. Maybe the positive transference he has developed for the head of the institute will play a positive part in stabilizing his psychic state.

How AIDS Hypochondria Functions as Relief and Defense

The fixation on the idea of suffering from a fatal disease like AIDS brought Heiner psychic relief due to various reasons. In the following, I will try to describe these reasons from Heiner's point of view. The goal is to make plausible why Heiner sticks so stubbornly to his hypochondriac ideas.

By seeing only AIDS as something that is threatening me, I have connected my anxiety to an object that my imagination can grasp, or at least understand better than my parents' contradictory and partially unexpressed expectations of me.

AIDS puts me into the position of someone persecuted by fate. Although I am convinced that I have become infected with AIDS through some moral failing and thus the disease is a just punishment, the others know nothing about that and therefore they have to spare me remonstrations and reproaches. As far as others know, I have done nothing to cause this illness.

This gives me the opportunity of letting out all my aggressions that should actually be directed towards my mother and father. But as this seems absolutely impossible to me, I direct all aggressions against myself, because I deserve to be punished and rejected for my moral failing.

Moreover, my fixed idea which no one wants to share with me makes me an independent person for the first time in my life. Whereas I am usually likely to shape my opinions according to my parents' or the majority's point of view, I can now prove my moral strength and stick to my ideas. I don't care that the price for finally stating my own opinions is rather high.

Maybe I am one of those men who manage everyday challenges by going with the flow. Secretly, I dream of being a strong man who sticks to his principles, the man my dad has pictured for me since I was a child, a man just like Superman. As a soccer player, I was able to make myself believe for quite a while that I was one of the tough guys. »I thought that people believed me that I am such a Rambo type of guy«. But given my complex family situation, I constantly have to navigate in order to avoid isolation and not cause my mother unbearable anxieties. Therefore, I secretly have to feel contempt for myself because I am constantly betraying my adopted ideal of manliness. I cannot direct my hatred against my father because he is stronger than me; I also cannot direct it against my mother because I feel like I depend on her and I could not take responsibility for her having a mental breakdown. It does, however, give me relief to direct all the hatred against myself and destroy myself, and I can thus indirectly express the immense hatred I harbor against my parents, who I am causing tremendous pain that way: I can make them feel guilty and symbolically say to them: Look, here is the monster into which you have made me!

By remaining immune from all attempts to talk me out of my fixed idea of an AIDS infection, I can create a sense of my-

self as a stable and autonomous person. It is possible that I am still unstable in everyday situations; this, however, offers me a chance to prove my ability to stand up for my beliefs and no argument can be logical enough to shake this idea of mine. Just the mere fact of having an opinion that others doubt and oppose makes me feel strong, brave and independent. The more people object to my disease, the more self-confident I feel. Everyone can see how weak I am and how badly I feel, and nobody can prove that I am not infected with a sort of HIV that has not yet been found, no matter how many tests they put me through. My doubting the absolute validity of the various AIDS tests puts me on the side of the greatest authorities in the field.

Compared to my inner feelings, my body is something that belongs to the outside. I experience my body as being less essential than my inner feelings and conflicts which make up the core of my ego and my personality. That is why I prefer to concentrate all my thoughts and feelings, including the feelings, comments and expectations of the people around me, on my body and my illness, not on me as a person, as if I were saying: I throw both my body and my disease at their feet and gain some freedom for myself by doing so. My illness protects me from their expectations and interference.

I might describe my AIDS hypochondria as some kind of defense corset that hides how useless I feel. AIDS justifies my desperation and depression, both of which are actually caused by my own person. By lamenting my AIDS infection, I can protect myself from feelings of inferiority that would actually be much more threatening.

The core of my problem is actually the fear of the breaking-down of my ego, the fear of its dissolution if I cut off my relationship with my mother. By projecting all my fears onto my body and my illness, I have found something to connect my anxiety to. That makes it easier to handle and less frightening. As a matter of fact, I often stick to the created fact of my AIDS infection without actually being frightened or sad. If we were to agree to see it this way, I am not anxious: in order to recover, I would probably have to be brave enough to feel the fear, the range and the sadness adequate to my inner life and my family situation.

So far the description of the unconscious and defensive meaning of the AIDS phobia from Heiner's point of view. But what meaning does his illness have for the family dynamics?

At first, Heiner's AIDS phobia shows that the collective neurotic defense system within the family has become unstable. As usual, the family therapist meets the family at a time when the character-neurotic family configuration is changing (cf. Richter 1970, p. 74). Throughout the years, the family had centered around the anxiety-neurotic mother in a way that her illness did not show. At the point where Heiner is taking steps in order to distance himself from the family, the incompatibility of his desire to gain independence with the family ideology becomes obvious. Heiner has had to suppress his separation and individuation wishes even more and punish himself for that. Nobody in the family is supposed to do anything that could endanger the mutual dependence, especially the dependence on the mother as the anxious leading figure. The family cannot risk to have anyone who is an odd-man-out seeking independence, because their character-neurotic armor is not based upon separation processes within the family but, on the contrary, upon solidarity according to the motto: »We are a closed society and live in beautiful harmony in our nursery-like world. Evil exists only on the outside«. Anyone who tries to separate himself from this unit destroys the family consensus and destabilizes the entire family-neurotic defense system. Heiner has had to pay for his ambitions with massive feelings of guilt and the development of an individual pathology.

The family, which has always stuck together pseudo-harmoniously, closed its eyes to violence, cruelty, hatred and injustice and projected all these things onto the outside world, is now being confronted with the fact that »evil«, namely, AIDS, has made its way right into their midst. In analyzing the family dynamics, we can say that Heiner's imagined AIDS infection brings back the suppressed family aggressions that had previously been projected onto the outside world. To summarize this idea, we can say the following: we can observe the return of the evil mother imago, or, extending this to a multi-generation perspective, the return of the suppressed evil grandmother imago.

Translated by Zvi Lothane

BIBLIOGRAPHY[1]

Aigner, J. C. (2001): Der ferne Vater. Gießen (Psychosozial-Verlag).

Akhtar, S. (1999): Immigration and Identity. Turmoil, Treatment, and Transformation. Northvale, New Jersey (Aronson).

Allport, G. W. (1954): The Nature of Prejudice. NY (Anchor).

Altmeyer, M. (2001): Nach dem Terror, vor dem Kreuzzug. Spekulationen über das Böse und seine Quellen. Kommune 19 (10), 11–15.

Arendt, H. (1958): Vita activa oder Vom tätigen Leben. München 1999 (Piper).

Arlow, J. A. (2000): The Hartmann Era. In: Bergmann, M. S. (Ed.) (2000): The Hartmann Era. New York (Other Press), pp. 81–88.

Auchter, T. (1978): Die Suche nach dem Vorgestern – Trauer und Kreativität. Psyche 32, 52–77.

Auchter, T. (1992): Fremdenangst als psychosoziale Störung. In: Streek, U. (Ed.): Das Fremde in der Psychoanalyse. New edition, Gießen 2001 (Psychosozial-Verlag), pp. 225–234.

Balint, M. (1959): Angstlust und Regression. Stuttgart (Klett).

Bauman, Z. (1993): Liquid Modernity. Cambridge, England (Polity Press).

Becker, N. (1996): Psychoanalytische Theorie sexueller Perversionen. In: Sigusch, V. (Ed.): Sexuelle Störungen und ihre Behandlung. Stuttgart (Thieme), pp. 222–240.

Bell, K., et al. (Eds.) (2002): Migration und Verfolgung. Psychoanalytische Perspektiven. Gießen (Psychosozial-Verlag).

Bergmann, M. S. (1987): Eine Geschichte der Liebe. Vom Umgang des Menschen mit einem rätselhaften Gefühl. Frankfurt 1999 (Fischer).

Bergmann, M. S. (Ed.) (2000a): The Hartmann Era. New York (Other Press).

Bergmann, M. S. (2000b): Der Konflikt zwischen Aufklärung und Romantik im Spiegel der Geschichte der Psychoanalyse. In: Jahrbuch der Psychoanalyse 42, Stuttgart, Bad Cannstatt (frommann-holzboog), pp. 773–103.

---

[1] As English translations of most of the German sources were not available, quotations from them were translated by the translators of the individual essays. This also applies to some of the quotations by Freud. Wherever English translations were used, they are listed in the bibliography.

Bergmann, M. S., Jucovy, M. E. & Kestenberg, J. S. (Eds.) (1982): Kinder der Opfer, Kinder der Täter. Psychoanalyse und Holocaust. Frankfurt (Fischer).

Berner, W. (1996): Imre Hermanns Anklammerung. Die Pädophilie und eine neue Sicht der Triebe. Psyche 50, 1036–1054.

Bettelheim, B. (1979, German 1980): Erziehung zum Überleben Frankfurt a. M. (Fischer).

Bettelheim, B. (1960, German 1964): Aufstand gegen die Masse. Die Chance des Individuums in der modernen Gesellschaft. Frankfurt a. M. (Fischer).

Blum, H. S. (2000): The Idealization of Theory and the Aim of Adaptation: The Passing of the Hartmann Enterprise and Era: In: Bergmann, M. S. (Ed.) (2000): The Hartmann Era. New York (Other Press), pp. 89–104.

Boetticher, D. von (1999): Meine Werke sind lauter Diagnosen. Über die ärztliche Dimension im Werk Arthur Schnitzlers. Heidelberg (Universitätsverlag C. Winter).

Bohleber, W. (1989): Psychoanalyse, romantische Naturphilosophie und deutsches idealistisches Denken. Psyche 43, 506–521.

Bohleber, W. (1992): Nationalismus, Fremdenhaß und Antisemitismus. Psychoanalytische Überlegungen. Psyche 46, 689–709.

Bohleber, W. (1994): Die Dynamik des Fremden. In: Hessische Stiftung für Friedens- und Konfliktforschung, Institut für Sozialforschung, Sigmund-Freud-Institut (1994): Rechtsextremismus und Fremdenfeindlichkeit in der demokratischen Gesellschaft. Konferenz vom 29. September bis 1. Oktober 1994 in Frankfurt/M. (Selbstverlag), pp. 383–396.

Böhme, H. & Böhme, G. (1996): Das Andere der Vernunft. Zur Entwicklung von Rationalitätsstrukturen am Beispiel Kants. Frankfurt (Suhrkamp).

Broder, H. M. (2001): Nur nicht provozieren! Der Spiegel 38, 169–170.

Brody, S. & Axelrad, S. (1970): Angst und Ichbildung in der Kindheit. Stuttgart 1974 (Klett-Cotta).

Büttner, C. (2002): Mit Gewalt ins Paradies. Psychologische Anmerkungen zu Terror und Terrorismus. HSFK Standpunkte 6 (2001).

Cairo-Chiarandini, I. (2001): Eine Sicht aus New York. IPA Newsletter 10 (2), 36.

Chasseguet-Smirgel, J. (1975): The Ego-Ideal. NY (Norton). German 1981: Das Ichideal. Psychoanalytischer Essay über die »Krankheit der Idealität«. Frankfurt a. M. (Suhrkamp).

Chasseguet-Smirgel, J. (1986): Creativity and Perversion. London (Free Association).

Cierpka, M. (1999): Das geschiedene Familiengefühl in Scheidungsfamilien. In: Schlösser, A.-M. & Höhfeld, K. (Eds.): Trennungen. Gießen (Psychosozial-Verlag), pp. 85–100.

Dahmer, H. (1971): Psychoanalyse und historischer Materialismus. In: Psychoanalyse als Sozialwissenschaft. Mit Beiträgen von Alfred Lorenzer, Helmut Dahmer, Klaus Horn, Karola Brede, Enno Schwanenberg. Frankfurt (Suhrkamp), pp. 60–92.

Devereux, G. (1978): Ethnopsychoanalysis. Psychoanalysis and Anthropology as Complementary Frames of Reference. Berkeley (University of California Press).

Devereux, G. (1980): Basic Problems of Ethnopsychiatry. Chicago (The University of Chicago Press).

Dohnanyi, K. von (1986): Eröffnungsrede zum 34. Kongress der Internationalen Psychoanalytischen Vereinigung am 28. Juli 1985. Psyche 40, 860–863.

Dornes, M. (1993): Der kompetente Säugling. Die präverbale Entwicklung des Menschen. Frankfurt (Fischer).

Dornes, M. (1996): Margaret Mahlers Theorie neu betrachtet. Psyche 50, 989–1018.

Düe, M. (1988): Freudsche Psychoanalyse im Widerstreit von Romantik und Aufklärung. Luzifer-Amor. Zeitschrift zur Geschichte der Psychoanalyse 1, 32–48.

Eckart, W. U. & Seidler, G. (in press): Möglichkeiten und Perspektiven einer historischen Traumaforschung (working title). Gießen (Psychosozial-Verlag).

Ellenberger, H. (1985): Die Entdeckung des Unbewußten. Zürich (Diogenes).

Erdheim, M. (1992a): Fremdeln. Kursbuch 107, pp. 19–32.

Erdheim, M. (1992b): Das Eigene und das Fremde. Psyche 46, 730–744.

Erdheim, M. & Blaser, A. (1998): Malend das Unbewußte erkunden. In: Arnold Böcklin, Giorgio de Chirico, Max Ernst. Eine Reise ins Ungewisse. Ausstellungskatalog. Bern (Benteli), pp. 194–202.

Erikson, E. H. (1950): Childhood and Society. NY (Norton).

Erikson, E. H. (1959): Identität und Lebenszyklus. 3 Aufsätze. Frankfurt a. M. (Suhrkamp).

Erikson, E. H. (1968): Identity: Youth and Crisis. NY (Norton).

Ermann, M. (1988): Aids-Phobie. Münch. med. Wschr. 130, 12–14.

Fallend, K. & Nitzschke, B. (Eds.) (2002): Der »Fall« Wilhelm Reich. Beiträge zum Verhältnis von Psychoanalyse und Politik. Gießen (Psychosozial-Verlag).

Fenichel, O. (1931): Perversionen, Psychosen, Charakterstörungen. Psychoanalytische spezielle Neurosenlehre. Wien (Internationaler Psychoanalytischer Verlag).

Ferenczi, S. (1933): Confusion of Tongues Between Adults and the Child. In: Balint, M. (Ed.): Final Contributions to the Theory and Technique of Psychoanalysis. London (Hogarth), pp. 156–167.

Ferenczi, S. & Rank, O. (1924): Entwicklungsziele der Psychoanalyse. Zur Wechselbeziehung von Theorie und Praxis. Leipzig, Wien, Zürich 1925 (Internationaler Psychoanalytischer Verlag). Reprint: Wien 1998 (Turia und Kant).

Fischer-Streek, A. (1992): Geil auf Gewalt. Psychoanalytische Bemerkungen zu Adoleszenz und Rechtsextremismus. Psyche 46, 745–768.

Fisher, D. J. (2003): Psychoanalytische Kulturkritik und die Seele des Menschen. Essays über Bruno Bettelheim. Gießen (Psychosozial-Verlag).

Floto, C., Fassl, H. & Hettwer, H. (1988): Aids-Prävention und öffentlicher Gesundheitsdienst. Öff. Gesundh.-Wes. 50, 641–646.

Freud, A. (1936): Das Ich und die Abwehrmechanismen. In: Die Schriften der Anna Freud. Bd. I. München 1980 (Kindler), pp. 193–355.

Freud, M. (1999): Mein Vater Sigmund Freud. Heidelberg (Mattes).

Freud, S. (1895): Studien über Hysterie. In: Freud GW, Bd. I, pp. 75–312.

Freud, S. (1900): Die Traumdeutung. In: Freud GW, Bd. II/III.

Freud, S. (1907): Der Wahn und die Träume in W. Jensens »Gradiva«. In: Freud GW, Bd. VII, pp. 31–128.

Freud, S. (1908): Der Dichter und das Phantasieren. In: Freud GW, Bd. VII, pp. 211–223.

Freud, S. (1910): Eine Kindheitserinnerung des Leonardo da Vinci. In: Freud GW, Bd. VIII, pp. 127–212.

Freud, S. (1913): Das Interesse an der Psychoanalyse. In: Freud GW, Bd. VIII. pp. 389–420.

Freud, S. (1914): On the History of the Psychoanalytic Movement. SE Vol. 14. New York (Norton).

Freud, S. (1915a): Vergänglichkeit. In: Freud GW Vol. X, pp. 357–361.

Freud, S. (1915b): Zeitgemäßes über Krieg und Tod. In: Freud GW Vol. X, pp. 323–355.

Freud, S. (1916): Trauer und Melancholie. In: Freud GW Bd. , pp. 427–446.

Freud, S. (1916/17): Introductory Lectures on Psycho-Analysis. SE Vols. 15 and 16. New York (Norton).

Freud, S. (1919): Das Unheimliche. In: Freud GW Bd. XII, pp. 227–268.

Freud, S. (1925): Die Widerstände gegen die Psychoanalyse. In: GW Bd. XIV, pp. 97–110.

Freud, S. (1926): Hemmung, Symptom und Angst. GW XIV, pp. 111–205.

Freud, S. (1927): Fetishism. SE 21, pp. 149–158.

Freud, S. (1928): Dostojewski und die Vatertötung. GW, Bd. XIV, pp. 397–418.

Freud, S. (1930): Civilization and its Discontents. SE Vol. 21. New York (Norton).

Freud, S. (1933): Neue Folge der Vorlesungen zur Einführung in die Psychoanalyse. GW, Bd. XV.

Freud, S. (1960): Briefe 1873–1939. Frankfurt (Fischer).

Freud, S. & Pfister, O. (1963): Briefe 1909–1939. Hg. von E. L. Freud und H. Meng. Frankfurt a. M. (Fischer).

Freud, S. & Zweig, A. (1968): Briefwechsel. Hg. von E. L. Freud. Frankfurt a. M. (Fischer).

Friedel, H. (Ed.) (1995): Der Kampf der Geschlechter. Der neue Mythos in der Kunst 1850–1930. Köln (DuMont).

Fromm, E. (1961): Den Vorrang hat der Mensch! Ein sozialistisches Manifest und Programm. GA Volume V, pp. 19–197.

Fromm, E. (1963): Der Ungehorsam als ein psychologisches und ethisches Problem. In: Erich Fromm GA, Bd. IX, pp. 367–373.

Fromm, E. (1964): Die Seele des Menschen. Ihre Fähigkeit zum Guten und zum Bösen. GA II, pp. 159–268.

Fromm, E. (1977): Freuds Modell des Menschen und seine gesellschaftlichen Determinanten. In: Erich Fromm Gesamtausgabe Bd. VIII, pp. 231–251.

Fürstenau, P. (1964): Ich-Psychologie und Anpassungsproblem. Eine Auseinandersetzung mit Heinz Hartmann. In: Jahrbuch der Psychoanalyse. Bd. 3, Bern und Stuttgart (Huber), pp. 30–55.

Fürstenau, P. (1967): »Sublimierung« in affirmativer und negativ-kritischer Anwendung. In: Jahrbuch der Psychoanalyse 4, pp. 43–62.

Gay, P. (1989): Freud. Eine Biographie für unsere Zeit. Frankfurt (Fischer).

Gehlen, A. (1963): Studien zur Anthropologie und Soziologie. Neuwied.

Gehlen, A. (1986): Der Mensch. Seine Natur und seine Stellung in der Welt. Wiesbaden (Aula).

Gödde, G. (1999): Traditionslinien des »Unbewußten«. Schopenhauer – Nietzsche – Freud. Tübingen (edition dicord).

Goldhagen, D. J. (1996): Hitler's Willing Executioners: Ordinary Germans and the Holocaust. NY (Knopf).

Grinberg, L. & Grinberg, R. (1984): Psychoanalyse der Migration und des Exils. München 1990 (Verlag Internationale Psychoanalyse).

Grunberger, B. (1984/1989): On Purity. In: Grunberger, B.: New Essays on Narcissism. London (Free Association Books), pp. 89–104.

Grunberger, B. & Dessuant, P. (1997/2000): Narzissmus, Christentum, Antisemitismus. Eine psychoanalytische Untersuchung. Stuttgart (Klett-Cotta).

Haubl, R., Lamott, F. & Traue, H. (Eds.) (2003): Über Lebensgeschichten. psychosozial Nr. 91, Heft I: Trauma und Erzählung.

Hartmann, H. (1937): Ich-Psychologie und Anpassungsproblem. Stuttgart 1960 (Klett).

Heitmeyer, W. (1992): Die Bielefelder Rechtsextremismus-Studie. Erste Langzeituntersuchung zur politischen Sozialisation männlicher Jugendlicher. München (Juventa).

Henseler, H. (1974): Narzißtische Krisen. Zur Psychodynamik des Selbstmords. Reinbek (Rowohlt).

Hermanns, L. (2001): Fünfzig Jahre Deutsche Psychoanalytische Vereinigung. Zur Geschichte der Psychoanalyse in Deutschland 1950 bis 2000. In: Bohleber, W. & Drews, S. (Eds.) (2001): Die Gegenwart der Psychoanalyse – die Psychoanalyse der Gegenwart. Stuttgart (Klett-Cotta).

Hilgers, M. (1996): Scham. Gesichter eines Affekts. Göttingen (Vandenhoeck & Ruprecht).

Hilgers, M. (2001a): Kranke Hirne. Psychosozial 24 (III), 107–108.

Hilgers, M. (2001b): Nationale Scham und ihre Folgen. Psychosozial 24 (III), 109–111.

Hirsch, M. (1989): Hypochondrie und Dysmorphophobie. In: Hirsch, M. (Ed.) (1989): Der eigene Körper als Objekt. Zur Psychodynamik selbstdestruktiven Körperagierens. Berlin (Springer), pp. 77 ff.

Hirsch, M. (Ed.) (1989/1998): Der eigene Körper als Objekt. Zur Psychodynamik selbstdestruktiven Körperagierens. New edition. Gießen (Psychosozial-Verlag).

Hirsch, M. (1996): Wege vom realen Trauma zur Autoaggression. Forum der Psychoanalyse 12, 31–44.

Hirschmann, K. (2001): Terrorismus in neuen Dimensionen. Hintergründe und Schlussfolgerungen. Aus Politik und Zeitgeschichte 51, 7–15.

Hole, G. (1995): Fanatismus. Der Drang zum Extrem und seine psychologischen Wurzeln. Freiburg (Herder).

Horn, K. (1970): Aspekte der Ich-Psychologie Heinz Hartmanns. Psyche 24, pp. 157–187.

Horn, K. (1971): Insgeheime kuturistische Tendenzen der modernen psychoanalytischen Orthodoxie. Zum Verhältnis von Subjektivem und Gesellschaftlichem in der Ich-psychologie. In: Psychoanalyse als Sozialwissenschaft. Mit Beiträgen von Alfred Lorenzer, Helmut Dahmer, Klaus Horn, Karola Brede, Enno Schwanenberg. Frankfurt

(Suhrkamp), pp. 93–151.

Jacobsen, K. (2000): Blaming Bettelheim. Psychoanalytic Revue 87, 385–415.

Jacoby, R. (1985): Die Verdrängung der Psychoanalyse oder Der Triumph des Konformismus. Frankfurt a. M. (Fischer).

Jäger, H. (1988) (Ed.): Aids-Phobie. Krankheitsbild und Behandlungsmöglichkeiten. Stuttgart (Thieme).

Janus, L. (1994): Otto Rank – der unentdeckte Pionier einer erweiterten Psychosomatik. In: Meyer, A.-E. & Lamparter, U. (Eds.) (1994): Pioniere der Psychosomatik. Beiträge zur Entwicklungsgeschichte einer ganzheitlichen Medizin. Heidelberg (Asanger), pp. 182–194.

Janus, L. (Ed.) (1998): Die Wiederentdeckung Otto Ranks für die Psychoanalyse. Schwerpunktthema von: psychosozial 73. Gießen (Psychosozial-Verlag).

Janus, L. & Wirth, H.-J. (2000): Einleitung zu Rank, O. (2000): Kunst und Künstler. Gießen (Psychosozial-Verlag).

Jones, E. (1957): Das Leben und Werk von Sigmund Freud. Bände I–III. Bern 1960 (Huber).

Kaufhold, R. (Ed.) (1993): Pioniere der Psychoanalytischen Pädagogik: Bruno Bettelheim, Rudolf Ekstein, Ernst Federn und Siegfried Bernfeld. psychosozial 53 (I/1993), 16. Jg.

Kaufhold, R. (Ed.) (1994): Annäherung an Bruno Bettelheim. Mainz (beim Autor für 12 Euro erhältlich).

Kaufhold, R. (Ed.) (1999): Ernst Federn: Versuche zur Psychologie des Terrors. Material zum Leben und Werk von Ernst Federn. Gießen (Psychosozial-Verlag).

Kaufhold, R. (2001): Bettelheim, Ekstein, Federn: Impulse für die psychoanalytisch-pädagogische Bewegung. Mit einem Vorwort von Ernst Federn. Gießen (Psychosozial-Verlag).

Kaufhold, R. (2003a): Spurensuche zur Geschichte der in die USA emigrierten Wiener Psychoanalytischen Pädagogen. Luzifer-Amor 31, 37–69.

Kaufhold, R. (2003b): Persönliche Mitteilung.

Kernberg, O. F. (1975/1980): Borderline-Störungen und pathologischer Narzißmus. Frankfurt (Suhrkamp).

Kernberg, O. (1992): Aggression in Personality Disorders and Perversions. New Haven, CT (Yale University Press).

Kernberg, O. (1998): Dreißig Methoden zur Unterdrückung der Kreativität von Kandidaten der Psychoanalyse. Psyche 52, 199–213.

Kernberg, O. F. (2002): Affekt, Objekt und Übertragung. Aktuelle Entwicklungen der psychoanalytischen Theorie und Technik. Gießen (Psychosozial-Verlag).

Kluge, F. (1989): Etymologisches Wörterbuch der deutschen Sprache. Berlin (de Gruyter).

Kohut, H. (1971): The Analysis of the Self. NY (International Universities Press).

Kohut, H. (1973): Überlegungen zum Narzißmus und zur narzisstischen Wut. Psyche 27, 513–554.

Kohut, H. (1981): Die Heilung des Selbst. Frankfurt (Suhrkamp).

Kollbrunner, J. (2001): Der kranke Freud. Stuttgart (Klett-Cotta).

Krüll, M. (1979): Freud und sein Vater. Die Entstehung der Psychoanalyse und Freuds ungelöste Vaterbindung. Frankfurt (Fischer) (1992).

Kunz, H. (1975): Grundfragen der psychoanalytischen Anthropologie. Göttingen (Vandenhoeck & Ruprecht).

Lachkar, J. (2002): The Psychological Make-up of a Suicide Bomber. The Journal of Psychohistory 28, 349–367.

Lockot, R. (2003): Erinnern und Durcharbeiten. Gießen (Psychosozial-Verlag).

Luczak, H. (2001): Die Macht, die aus der Ohnmacht kommt. Geo Epoche. Das Magazin für Geschichte. Schwerpunktthema: Der 11. September 2001, 7, 86–91.

Mahler, M. S. (1972): On the First Three Subphases of the Separation-Individuation Process. International Journal of Psychoanalysis 53, 333–338.

Mahler, M. S. (1985): Studien über die drei ersten Lebensjahre. Stuttgart (Klett-Cotta).

Marquard, O. (1987): Transzendentaler Idealismus, romantische Naturphilosophie, Psychoanalyse. Köln (Verlag für Philosophie).

Menaker, E. (1997): Schwierige Loyalitäten. Psychoanalytische Lehrjahre in Wien 1930–1935. Gießen (Psychosozial-Verlag).

Mertens, W. (1981): Psychoanalyse. Stuttgart (Kohlhammer).

Mertens, W. (1992): Entwicklung der Psychosexualität und der Geschlechtsidentität. Bd. 1: Geburt bis 4. Lebensjahr. Stuttgart (Kohlhammer).

Mitchell, S. (2003): Bindung und Beziehung. Relationales Denken in der Psychoanalyse. Gießen (Psychosozial-Verlag).

Mitscherlich, A. (1981): Das persönliche und das soziale Ich. Ein Lesebuch. München (Piper).

Möhring, P. (1985): »Die Schicksalshaut«. Eine Studie zu Sigmund Freuds Krankheiten. Psycho-Analyse 2+3 (Bonz), 123–152.

Moses, R. & Eickhoff, F.-W. (Eds.) (1992): Die Bedeutung des Holocaust für nicht direkt Betroffene. Jahrbuch der Psychoanalyse. Beiheft 14. Stuttgart-Bad Cannstatt (Frommann-Holzboog).

Mühlleitner, E. (1992): Biographisches Lexikon der Psychoanalyse.

Tübingen (edition discord).

Mühlleitner, E. & Reichmayr, J. (2003): Die »Wiener« Psychoanalyse im Exil. Luzifer-Amor 31, 70–105.

Müller-Braunschweig, H. (1974): Psychopathologie und Kreativität. Psyche 28, 600–634.

Müller-Braunschweig, H. (1984): Aspekte einer psychoanalytischen Kreativitätstheorie. In: Kraft, H. (Ed.) (1984): Psychoanalyse, Kunst und Kreativität heute. Die Entwicklung der analytischen Kunstpsychologie seit Freud. Köln (DuMont), pp. 122–145.

Neckel, S. (1991): Status und Scham. Zur symbolischen Reproduktion sozialer Ungleichheit. Frankfurt (Campus).

Neraal, T. (1988): Der irrationale Anteil der Aids-Ansteckungsangst. In: Jäger, H. (1988) (Ed.): Aids-Phobie. Krankheitsbild und Behandlungsmöglichkeiten. Stuttgart (Thieme), pp. 68–72.

Nicklas, A. (1988): Die politische Funktion von Feindbildern. Thesen zum subjektiven Faktor in der Politik. In: Sommer, G. et al. (Eds.): Feindbilder im Dienste der Aufrüstung. Beiträge aus Psychologie und anderen Humanwissenschaften. Schriftenreihe des Arbeitskreises Marburger Wissenschaftler für Friedens- und Abrüstungsforschung Nr. 3. Marburg (Eigenverlag), pp. 32–36.

Nicklas, A. (1994): Kulturelle Identität und Ausländerfeindschaft. In: Hessische Stiftung für Friedens- und Konfliktforschung, Institut für Sozialforschung, Sigmund-Freud-Institut (1994): Rechtsextremismus und Fremdenfeindlichkeit in der demokratischen Gesellschaft. Konferenz vom 29. September bis 1. Oktober 1994 in Frankfurt/M. (Selbstverlag), pp. 43–62.

Nitzschke, B. (2001): »Warum hat keiner von all den Frommen die Psychoanalyse geschaffen ...?« Sigmund Freuds transkulturelles Erbe. http//www.psychosozial-verlag.de.

Nitzschke, B. (2003): Persönliche Mitteilung.

Piven, J. S. (2002): On the Psychosis (Religion) of Terrorists. In: Piven, J., Ziolo, P. & Lawton, H. (Eds.): Terror and Apocalypse: Psychological Undercurrents of History Volume II. NY (iUniverse/Bloomusalem), pp. 153–204.

Plassmann, R. (1989): Artifizielle Krankheiten und Münchhausen-Syndrom. In: Hirsch, M. (Ed.) (1989/1998): Der eigene Körper als Objekt. Zur Psychodynamik selbstdestruktiven Körperagierens. New edition. Gießen (Psychosozial-Verlag), pp. 118–154.

Plessner, H. (1928): Die Stufen des Organischen und der Mensch. Frankfurt (Suhrkamp).

Rank, O. (1907): Der Künstler. Wien (Hugo Heller). Vierte, vermehrte Auflage unter dem Titel: Der Künstler und andere Beiträge zur Psychoanalyse des dichterischen Schaffens. Leipzig, Wien, Zürich 1925

(Internationaler Psychoanalytischer Verlag).

Rank, O. (1909): Der Mythos von der Geburt des Helden. Versuch einer psychologischen Mythendeutung. Zweite, wesentlich erweiterte Auflage (1922), Leipzig, Wien (Deuticke).

Rank, O. (1911): Die Lohengrin-Sage. Ein Beitrag zu ihrer Motivgestaltung und Deutung. Leipzig, Wien (Deuticke).

Rank, O. (1912): Das Inzest-Motiv in Dichtung und Sage. Grundzüge einer Psychologie des dichterischen Schaffens. Zweite, wesentlich vermehrte und verbesserte Auflage (1925), Leipzig, Wien (Deuticke).

Rank, O. (1914): Der Doppelgänger. Eine psychoanalytische Studie. (Zuerst in: Imago III. Band, 1914), Leipzig, Wien, Zürich 1925 (Internationaler Psychoanalytischer Verlag). Reprint: Wien 1993 (Turia und Kant).

Rank, O. (1919): Psychoanalytische Beiträge zur Mythenforschung. Leipzig, Wien, Zürich (Internationaler Psychoanalytischer Verlag).

Rank, O. (1922): Die Don Juan-Gestalt. Leipzig, Wien, Zürich (Internationaler Psychoanalytischer Verlag).

Rank, O. (1924): Das Trauma der Geburt und seine Bedeutung für die Psychoanalyse. Leipzig, Wien, Zürich (Internationaler Psychoanalytischer Verlag). New edition: Gießen 1998 (Psychosozial-Verlag).

Rank, O. (2000): Kunst und Künstler. Erstpublikation des Urmanuskriptes von 1932 mit einer Einleitung von L. Janus und H.-J. Wirth. Gießen (Psychosozial-Verlag).

Rank, O. & Sachs, H. (1913): Die Bedeutung der Psychoanalyse für die Geisteswissenschaften. Amsterdam 1965 (Bonset).

Rauchfleisch, U. (1990): Psychoanalytische Betrachtungen zur musikalischen Kreativität. Psyche 44, 1113–1140.

Reichmayr, J. (1990): Spurensuche in der Geschichte der Psychoanalyse. Frankfurt a. M. (Stroemfeld).

Reichmayr, J. & Mühlleitner, E. (Eds.) (1998): Otto Fenichel 119 Rundbriefe, Bd. I (Europa) und II (Amerika). Frankfurt a. M. (Stroemfeld).

Richter, H.-E. (1963): Eltern, Kind und Neurose. Zur Psychoanalyse der kindlichen Rolle. Reinbek (Rowohlt).

Richter, H.-E. (1970): Patient Familie. Entstehung, Struktur und Therapie von Konflikten in Ehe und Familie. Reinbek (Rowohlt).

Richter, H.-E. (1976/1998): Flüchten oder Standhalten. New edition Gießen (Psychosozial-Verlag).

Richter, H.-E. (1978/1996): Zur Psychologie des Friedens. New edition Gießen (Psychosozial-Verlag).

Richter, H.-E. (1979): Der Gotteskomplex. Die Geburt und die Krise des Glaubens an die Allmacht des Menschen. Reinbek (Rowohlt).

Richter, H.-E. (1987): Gesellschaftliche Auswirkungen von Aids. Statement für die Sitzung der Enquete-Kommission des Deutschen Bundestages »Gefahren von Aids und wirksame Wege zu ihrer Eindämmung« vom 29. 9. 1987 in Bonn.

Richter, H.-E. (1992): Umgang mit Angst. Hamburg (Hoffmann & Campe).

Richter, H.-E. (1995): Psychoanalyse und Politik. Neuausgabe Gießen 2002 (Psychosozial-Verlag).

Richter, H.-E. (2002): Das Ende der Egomanie. Die Krise des westlichen Bewusstseins. Köln (Kiepenheuer & Witsch).

Richter, H.-E. & Beckmann, D. (1969/1986): Herzneurose. Stuttgart, New York (Thieme).

Rodewig, K. (Ed.) (2000): Identität, Integration und psychosoziale Gesundheit. Gießen (Psychosozial-Verlag).

Rosenfeld, H. (1964): The Psychopathology of Hypochondry. In: Rosenfeld, H. (1981): Psychotic States: A Psychoanalytical Approach. London (Karnac).

Rosenfeld, H. (1987): The psychotic Aspects of Personality. London (Karnac).

Rotmann, M. (1978): Die Triangulierung der frühkindlichen Sozialbeziehung. Psyche 32, 1105–1147.

Roy, A. (2001): Wut ist der Schlüssel. Ein Kontinent brennt – Warum der Terrorismus nur ein Symptom ist. Frankfurter Allgemeine Zeitung 9/28/2001, p. 49.

Sachsse, U. (1989): Blut tut gut. Genese, Psychodynamik und Psychotherapie offener Selbstbeschädigungen der Haut. In: Hirsch, M. (Ed.) (1989/1998): Der eigene Körper als Objekt. Zur Psychodynamik selbstdestruktiven Körperagierens. New edition. Gießen (Psychosozial-Verlag), pp. 94–117.

Safranski, R. (1994): Ein Meister aus Deutschland. Heidegger und seine Zeit. München (Hanser).

Safranski, R. (1997): Das Böse oder Das Drama der Freiheit. München (Hanser).

Schafer, R. (1972): Die psychoanalytische Anschauung der Realität (II). Psyche 26, 952–973.

Scheeler, M. (1926): Der Mensch als der sorgenvolle Protestant. In: Scheeler, M. (1994): Schriften zur Anthropologie. Stuttgart (Reclam), pp. 114–121.

Schilder, P. (1926): Selbstbeobachtung und Hypochondrie. In: Almanach der Psychoanalyse. Wien (Internationaler Psychoanalytischer Verlag), 190–197.

Schirra, B. (2001): Die Schüler des Terrors. Die Zeit No. 51, 12/13/2001, pp. 15–18.

Secord, P. F. & Backman, C. W. (1974): Sozial-Psychologie. Frankfurt (Fachbuchhandlung für Psychologie).

Sloterdijk, P. (1998): Sphären I. Blasen. Frankfurt (Suhrkamp).

Sloterdijk, P. (1999): Sphären II. Globen. Frankfurt (Suhrkamp).

Sontag, S. (1989): Aids und seine Metaphern. München (Hanser).

Spitz, R. (1965): Vom Säugling zum Kleinkind. Stuttgart (Klett).

Stadler, F. (Ed.) (1988): Vertriebene Vernunft, Bd. II. Emigration und Exil österreichischer Wissenschaft, Wien, München (Jugend und Volk).

Stein, A. & Stein, H. (1987): Kreativität. Psychoanalytische und philosophische Aspekte. Fellbach-Oeffingen (Bonz).

Sterba, R. (1985): Erinnerungen eines Wiener Psychoanalytikers. Frankfurt a. M. (Fischer).

Stern, M. (1974): Trauma, Todesangst und Furcht vor dem Tod. Psyche 26, 902–928.

Stierlin, H. (1978): Delegation und Familie. Beiträge zum Heidelberger Familiendynamischen Konzept. Frankfurt (Suhrkamp).

Stoller, R. J. (1979): Sexual Excitement: Dynamics of Erotic Life. NY (Pantheon).

Strenger, C. (1989): The classic and the romantic vision in Psychoanalysis. International Journal of Psycho-Analysis 70, 593–610.

Sznaider, N. (2001): Holocausterinnerung und Terror im globalen Zeitalter. Aus Politik und Zeitgeschichte B 52–53, 23–28.

Theweleit, K. (1977): Männerphantasien. 1. Band. Frauen, Fluten, Körper, Geschichte. Frankfurt (Roter Stern).

Theweleit, K. (1978): Männerphantasien. 2. Band. Männerkörper. Zur Psychoanalyse des weißen Terrors. Frankfurt (Roter Stern).

Timms, E. & Segal, N. (Eds.) (1988): Freud in Exile. Psychoanalysis and its Vicissitudes, New Haven, London (Yale University Press).

Uexküll, T. v. (1974): Psychosomatische Medizin. München (Urban u. Schwarzenberg).

Vollmoeller, W. (1988): Zum Thema Aids in der Psychiatrie und Psychotherapie: Spezielle psychodynamische und psychopathologische Aspekte anhand eines Falles mit »Aids-Phobie«. Zeitschrift für psychosomatische Medizin 34, 351–360.

Wahl, K. (1994): Gewalt und Fremdenfeindlichkeit – Jugendprobleme? In: Hessische Stiftung für Friedens- und Konfliktforschung, Institut für Sozialforschung, Sigmund-Freud-Institut (1994): Rechtsextremismus und Fremdenfeindlichkeit in der demokratischen Gesellschaft. Konferenz vom 29. September bis 1. Oktober 1994 in Frankfurt/M. (Selbstverlag), pp. 157–168.

Waldmann, P. (1998): Terrorismus. Provokation der Macht. München (Gerling Akademie).

Waldmann, P. (2001): »Das spricht für sich«. Die neue Dimension des Terrorismus: Die Täter benutzen die ganze Welt als Resonanzraum. Die tageszeitung, 12/27/2001, p. 4.

Weizsäcker, C. F. von (1967): Friedlosigkeit als seelische Krankheit. In: Der bedrohte Friede. Politische Aufsätze 1945–1981. München (dtv).

Whitebook, J. (1996): Sublimierung: ein »Grenzbegriff«. Psyche 50, 850–880.

Winnicott, D. W. (1965/1976): The Maturational Processes and the Facilitating Environment. London (Hogarth).

Wirth, H.-J. (1991): Deutsche Feigheit oder Mut zur Angst? Sozialpsychologische Betrachtungen zum Krieg am Golf. Vorgänge II, 614.

Wirth, H.-J. (2000): Spaltungsprozesse in der psychoanalytischen Bewegung und ihre Auswirkungen auf die Theoriebildung. In: Schlösser, A.-M. & Höhfeld, K. (Eds.) (2000): Psychoanalyse als Beruf. Gießen (Psychosozial-Verlag), pp. 177–192.

Wirth, H.-J. (2001): Versuch, den Umbruch von 68 und das Problem der Gewalt zu verstehen. In: Wirth, H.-J. (Ed.) (2001): Hitlers Enkel – oder Kinder der Demokratie? Die 68er-Generation, die RAF und die Fischer-Debatte. Gießen (Psychosozial-Verlag).

Wirth, H.-J. (2002): Narzissmus und Macht: Zur Psychoanalyse psychischer Störungen in der Politik. Gießen (Psychosozial-Verlag).

Wirth, H.-J. (2003): Family Dynamics and AIDS Phobia: A Case Study. Journal of Applied Psychoanalytic Studies. Special Issue on Psychoanalytic Couple and Family Therapy edited by David E. Scharff, M. D. & Jill Savege Scharff, M. D.

Wirth, H.-J. (2004): Psychoanalytic Thoughts on 9/11. Journal of Psycho-Social Studies Vol. 3 (1) No 4. www.btinternet.com/~psycho_social/Vol4/JPSS4_HJW1.htm

Wittenberger, G. (1995): Das »geheime Komitee« Sigmund Freuds. Tübingen (edition diskord).

Woidera, R. & Brosig, B. (1990): Aids-Hypochondrie. Intrapsychische und intrafamiliäre Konstellationen. In: Wirsching, M. & Richter, H.-E. (1990): Neues Denken in der Psychosomatik? Frankfurt (Fischer).

Woodward, Bob (2003): Bush at war. Amerika im Krieg. München (dva).

Worbs, M. (1983): Nervenkunst. Literatur und Psychoanalyse im Wien der Jahrhundertwende. Frankfurt (Europäische Verlagsanstalt).

Wurmser, L. (1987): Flucht vor dem Gewissen. Analyse von Über-Ich und Abwehr bei schweren Neurosen. Berlin, Heidelberg (Springer).

Wurmser, L. (1989): Die zerbrochene Wirklichkeit. Psychoanalyse als das Studium von Konflikt und Komplementarität. Berlin (Springer).

Yalom, I. D. (1989): Existenzielle Psychotherapie. Köln (Edition Humanistische Psychologie).

Index of Illustrations

INDEX OF PREVIOUS PUBLICATIONS
OF THE FOLLOWING MATERIAL

9/11 As A Collective Trauma was originally published as the chapter »Zeitgemäßes über Terrorismus, Krieg und Tod« in: Wirth, H.-J.: Narzissmus und Macht. Zur Psychoanalyse seelischer Störungen in der Politik. Giessen 2002 (Psychosozial-Verlag), pp. 362–391.

English versions of this article were previously published in:

1. The Journal of Psychohistory. Vol 30 No 4, 2003, 363–388.
2. Piven, J. S., Boyd, C. & Lawton, H. W. (Eds.): Jihad and Sacred Vengeance. Psychological Undercurrents of History. Volume III. New York, Lincoln, Shanghai 2002 (Writers Club), pp. 40–75.
3. Piven, J. S., Boyd, C. & Lawton, H. W. (Eds.): Terrorism, Jihad, and Sacred Vengeance. Giessen 2004 (Psychosozial-Verlag), pp. 137–165.
4. Journal of Psycho-Social Studies Vol 3 (1) No 4, 2004.
5. Piven, J. S. (Ed.) (2004): The Psychology of Death in Fantasy and History. Westport, Connecticut and London (Praeger), pp. 177–201.

Xenophobia and Violence as a Family and Psychosocial Disease was originally published under the title »Fremdenhaß und Gewalt als psychosoziale Krankheit« in: Psyche 55. Jhg., Heft 11, 2001, 1217–1244.

English versions of this article were previously published in:

1. Piven, J. S. Boyd, C. & Lawton, H. W. (Eds.): Jihad and Sacred Vengeance. Psychological Undercurrents of History.

Volume III. New York, Lincoln, Shanghai 2002 (Writers Club), pp. 189–225.
2. Piven, J. S. Boyd, C. & Lawton, H. W. (Eds.): Terrorism, Jihad, and Sacred Vengeance. Giessen 2004 (Psychosozial-Verlag), pp. 237–264.

Emigration, Biography und Psychoanalysis. The Story of Jewish Psychoanalysts who emigrated to the United States of America was originally published under the title »Emigration, Biographie und Psychoanalyse. Emigrierte Psychoanalytiker-Innen in Amerika« in: Bruder, H.-J. (Hg.): Die biographische Wahrheit ist nicht zu haben. Psychoanalyse und Biographieforschung. Giessen 2003 (Psychosozial-Verlag), pp. 221–248.

The Idea of Man in Psychoanalysis: Creator of his own Life or Subject to the Dark Instinctual Side of Human Nature? was originally published under the title »Das Menschenbild der Psychoanalyse: Kreativer Schöpfer des eigenen Lebens oder Spielball dunkler Triebnatur?« in: Schlösser, A. & Gerlach, A. (Hg.): Kreativität und Scheitern. Gießen 2001 (Psychosozial-Verlag), pp. 13–40.
Various English versions of this article were previously published in:
1. The Psychoanalytic Review. Special Issue on Death edited by Jerry S. Piven, Vol 90, Number 4, August 2003.
2. Creativity and Death in Psychoanalysis. In: Piven, J. S. (Ed.) (2004): The Psychology of Death in Fantasy and History. Westport, Connecticut and London (Praeger), pp. 137–162.

About Family Dynamics and the AIDS Phobia. A Case Study was originally published under the title »Zur Familiendynamik der Aids-Phobie. Eine Fallstudie« in: Möhring, P. & Neraal, T. (Eds.): Psychoanalytisch orientierte Familien- und Sozialtherapie. Das Gießener Konzept in der Praxis. Wiesbaden 1990 (Westdeutscher Verlag), pp. 249–264.

A shorter version of this article was previously published in: Applied Psychoanalysis. Special Issue on Psychoanalytic Couple and Family Therapy, edited by David E. Scharff, M. D. & Jill Savege Scharff, M. D., 2003.

ABOUT THE AUTHOR

Hans-Jürgen Wirth is a psychoanalyst and analytic family therapist, practicing in his own private practice. Member of the German Psychoanalytical Association (DPV) and the International Psychanalytic Association (IPA). Private university lecturer in the field of »Psychoanalysis with Special Emphasis on Prevention, Psychotherapy and Psychoanalytic Social Psychology« at the Department of Human and Health Sciences at the University of Bremen. University lecturer of psychoanalysis, depth-psychologically founded psychotherapy and psychoanalytically oriented family and social therapy at the *Institute for Psychoanalysis and Psychotherapy Giessen e. V.*, a member institute of the German Psychoanalytical Association (DPV).

Publisher and owner of the publishing houses Psychosozial-Verlag and Haland & Wirth. Editor of the German book series »Bibliothek der Psychoanalyse« (Psychosozial-Verlag), editor-in-chief of the journal *psychosozial*, author of numerous articles and books on the application of psychoanalysis. Recently published books: *Hitlers Enkel oder Kinder der Demokratie? Die 68-Generation, die RAF und die Fischer-Debatte*, Giessen 2001 (Psychosozial-Verlag), *Narzissmus und Macht. Zur Psychoanalyse seelischer Störungen in der Politik*, Giessen 2002 (Psychosozial-Verlag).

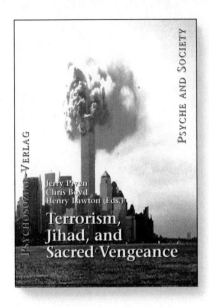

2003 · 378 Seiten· Broschur
EUR (D) 29,90 · SFr 52,20
ISBN 3-89806-282-1

Terrorism, Jihad, and Sacred Vengeance delves into the psychology of terrorism and religious violence. What comprise the ideas, impulses and fantasies of terrorists and suicide bombers? How do victimization and exposure to death affect the psyche? From fascistic and paranoid responses following September 11th, 2001, to dreams of entering Paradise and blissfully joining God through acts of self-destruction, to the symbolism of evil and sacrifice, Terrorism, Jihad, and Sacred Vengeance explores the madness and despair persisting in the wake of recent events.

P🌀V
Psychosozial-Verlag

Jörn W. Scheer (Ed.)

The Person in Society

Challenges to a
Constructivist Theory

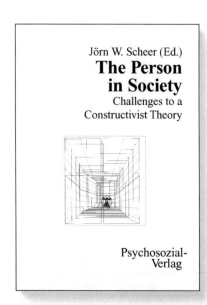

Psychosozial-
Verlag

2000 · 455 Seiten · Broschur
EUR (D) 22,90 · SFr 40,–
ISBN 3-89806-015-2

George A. Kelly's ground-breaking work „The Psychology of Personal Constructs" which preceded the „cognitive turn" in modern empirical psychology, stressed the importance of the meanings that individuals attach to persons and events in the world surrounding them. It introduced Repertory-Grid-Technique as the prime research tool to explore these individual meanings. During the first 30 years after the publication in 1955, the impact of the theory was largely restricted to the English speaking world.

The foundation of the „European Personal Construct Association" has provided a forum for the exchange of research findings and practical applications of the theory from different countries. This volume assembles reports on recent developments in theory and methodology as well as research findings from fields such as clinical psychology, psychiatry, education and organisational development.

P🔲V
Psychosozial-Verlag

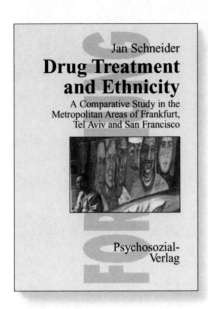

Jan Schneider
Drug Treatment and Ethnicity
A Comparative Study in the
Metropolitan Areas of Frankfurt,
Tel Aviv and San Francisco

Psychosozial-
Verlag

2001 · 289 Seiten · Broschur
EUR (D) 29,90 · Sfr 52,20
ISBN 3-89806-079-9

Developing multicultural competencies within the social services has been a continuous issue in recent years, however, there is a scarcity of concepts and knowledge as to how such relevance in service-delivery can be accomplished. The German, Israeli and American societies are subject of this comparative empirical study, which aims at clarifying the way in which these »modern, Western Welfare States« respond to ethnic minority populations in need of substance abuse treatment services. Not only does it present a systematic juxtaposition of differing drug treatment systems, drug prevalence rates and issues of immigration and ethnicity in these three countries; the conceptual framework illuminates paradigmatic ways in which substance abuse services and professionals can gain sensitivity towards the various ethnic groups differing from mainstream society.

P🏛V
Psychosozial-Verlag

»Ein Meisterwerk politischer Psychoanalyse«

Besondere Empfehlung für die Sachbuch-Bestenliste der Süddeutschen Zeitung, des NDR und des BuchJournals

Hans-Jürgen Wirth
Narzissmus und Macht
Zur Psychoanalyse seelischer Störungen in der Politik

2002
439 Seiten · gebunden
EUR (D) 24,90 · SFr 42,30
ISBN 3-89806-044-6

»Die Fallstudien, die Wirth auf Grund genauer Recherchen zur Barschel-Affäre, zu Helmut Kohl (mit zurückhaltendem Einbezug des Freitods von Hannelore Kohl), zur 68er Generation und zu Joschka Fischers stupenden Metamorphosen sowie zu Slobodan Milosevics Paranoia vorlegt, sind sehr ergiebig, besonders eindrucksvoll im Falle Uwe Barschels.«

Ludger Lütkehaus, NZZ

»Harte Bandagen also, die – so Wirth – dennoch nicht zu Politikverdrossenheit verleiten sollten: Erst wenn Bürger und Wähler den ›Einfluss unbewusster psychischer Konflikte auf Entscheidungen höchster Tragweite‹ erkennen würden, könnten ihnen Politik und Politiker wieder ›ein Stückchen näher‹ rücken.«

Der Standard

»Hans-Jürgen Wirth hat die Plattform erreicht, auf der eine allgemeine Psychoanalyse der Politik errichtet werden kann. Der Schritt war unerlässlich.«

Paul Parin

P🗟V
Psychosozial-Verlag